THE JEWISH PEOPLE

HISTORY • RELIGION • LITERATURE

THE JEWISH PEOPLE

HISTORY • RELIGION • LITERATURE

Advisory Editor
Jacob B. Agus

Editorial Board
Louis Jacob
Jacob Petuchowski
Seymour Siegel

THE MEMOIRS

OF

BER OF BOLECHOW

(1723—1805)

TRANSLATED FROM THE ORIGINAL HEBREW MS
WITH AN INTRODUCTION, NOTES AND A MAP

BY

M. VISHNITZER

ARNO PRESS
A New York Times Company
NEW YORK • 1973

Reprint Edition 1973 by Arno Press Inc.

Reprinted from a copy in
  The Hebrew Union College Library

THE JEWISH PEOPLE: History, Religion, Literature
ISBN for complete set: 0-405-05250-2
See last pages of this volume for titles.

Manufactured in the United States of America

———————◆———————

Library of Congress Cataloging in Publication Data

Ber, of Bolechow, 1723-1805.
    The memoirs of Ber of Bolechow.

    (The Jewish people: history, religion, literature)
    Reprint of the 1922 ed. published by Oxford
University Press, London.
    1. Jews in Bolechow. 2. Bolechow--History.
I. Wischnitzer, Mark, 1882-1955, ed. II. Title.
III. Series.
DS135.P62B623 1973   301.45'19'2404771   73-2186
ISBN 0-405-05252-9

THE MEMOIRS

OF

BER OF BOLECHOW

THE MEMOIRS

OF

BER OF BOLECHOW

(1723—1805)

TRANSLATED FROM THE ORIGINAL HEBREW MS
WITH AN INTRODUCTION, NOTES AND A MAP

BY

DR. M. VISHNITZER

HUMPHREY MILFORD
OXFORD UNIVERSITY PRESS
LONDON   EDINBURGH   GLASGOW
NEW YORK   TORONTO   MELBOURNE   CAPE TOWN
BOMBAY   CALCUTTA   MADRAS   SHANGHAI
1922

PRINTED BY ADOLF HOLZHAUSEN
IN VIENNA (AUSTRIA).

PREFACE.

The Memoirs of Ber of Bolechow or Ber Birkenthal, a Polish Jew, who lived during the period 1723—1805, are preserved in the Library of Jews' College, London.[1] It cannot be established how and whence the manuscript reached the College. A few small extracts from it were published by Dr. A. Marmorstein in 1913[2] and several other fragments by Dr. L. Lewin in 1916.[3] The present publication is the first complete edition in English.[4] The manuscript consists of 95 sheets, 21×13 cm., covered with modern eighteenth-century Hebrew cursive script. Its subject-matter consists of autobiographical records, descriptions of Jewish life, accounts of Polish affairs, information as to economic activities, family chronicles, stray thoughts concerning literary and social matters, and fragments of renderings of German and Polish historical works into Hebrew — the whole forming a series of disconnected chapters, without any attempt at systematic arrangement.

The first four pages give some extracts (in Hebrew) from a once famous book, the *Relazioni universali* of Giovanni Benesius Botero, which became known to Ber in a Polish translation; the next nine pages transfer us to another historical work — Humphrey Prideaux's *Old and New Testament* etc., a book which Ber valued highly and

[1] Nr. 31 of the manuscripts of the Library.

[2] *Die Memoiren Beer Bolechows*, in *Zeitschrift für Hebräische Bibliographie*, XVI.

[3] See *Jahrbuch der Jüdisch-Literarischen Gesellschaft*, Frankfurt (on the Main), vol. XI, 1916.

[4] The Hebrew original, which I am editing separately, appears simultaneously with the present publication, in Berlin.

a*

undertook to render into Hebrew. The subject again
changes on p. 14 of the manuscript, where an indignant
outburst against the slanderers of the Jewish faith is
followed by the author's recollections of the part which
he played in 1759 in the dispute with the Frankists.[1]
On that occasion he was presented by one of the nobles
among the audience with a copy of Botero's book, several
paragraphs of which occupy pp. 15—24 of the Jews'
College manuscript. Then follow different chapters from
Prideaux's work, which occupy altogether 18 pages of
the manuscript, being once interrupted (on p. 34) by an
excursus into Ber's literary plans. The actual Memoirs
of our author commence only on p. 43, and commence
for us with the end of a sentence, the beginning of which,
owing to the loss of the preceding page, remains unknown.
The author's narrative of his life and times runs on to
p. 190, but here also there is neither consecutiveness nor
chronological order. The narrative as we have it consists
of six unequal fragments, most of which start in the middle
of a sentence, while some end in the same manner. The
author frequently refers to parts of his story which are lost.

The present publication begins with p. 43 of the manuscript, and follows closely the order of the manuscript
pages.[2] It includes also the few autobiographical notes
scattered throughout the first 42 pages, which contain

[1] The Frankists were the partisans of Jacob Frank, who founded a semi-
Christian religious sect about the middle of the eighteenth century. See
S. Dubnow in the *Jewish Encyclopaedia*, vol. VI, where the literature on
this movement is given. Recent contributions towards the history of Frank
and his sects have been made by M. Vishnitzer, *The Epistle of the Frankists
in 1800* (R) in *Mémoires de l'Académie Impériale des Sciences de St. Péters-
bourg, VIII Série, Classe Historico-philologique*, vol. XII, Nr. 3, 1914; idem,
The Frankist Movement (R), in the *History of the Jewish People* (R), 1914,
vol. XI, chapter 15; Dr. A. Brawer, *A New Source for the History of Frank
and his Sect* (H.), in the Hebrew monthly *Hashiloah*, vol. 33, pp. 146—157,
330—343, 439—449; vol. 38, pp. 16—21, 231—238, 349—354, 446—457.

[2] Several passages occur twice. It thus appears that another copy of the
manuscript was made, or that the author himself had partly rewritten his
Memoirs.

otherwise only translations from printed books, and are therefore not worth reproducing.

Ber wrote a work on Jewish sectarian movements, entitled *Dibré Binah* (Words of Reason), which has been only recently discovered and published in part by Dr. A. Brawer.[1] This work not only includes autobiographical details which are not mentioned in the Memoirs, but also adds to our knowledge of Ber's literary and social activities; and I have drawn on it considerably in the Introduction to the present volume.

With a view to making the Memoirs of Ber intelligible to non-Jewish readers, I have provided the text with ample explanatory footnotes. The table of contents, the index to personal and geographical names, and the map will facilitate the use of the work.

Ber's style is not always very careful and correct from the literary or even from the grammatical point of view. It has therefore been necessary to amplify defective phrases in order to make them intelligible to the English reader. Words which I have added are put in brackets. Where the author dates an event (as he generally does) by the Jewish system, which reckons *anno mundi*,[2] I have added in brackets the date according to the common era.[3]

Biblical names occurring in the Memoirs are given in the spelling of the Revised Version of the English Bible. In the case of names which, like Ḥayyim, Naḥman, etc., are of post-Biblical origin I have followed the rules adopted by Neubauer in his *Catalogue of the Hebrew Manuscripts in the Bodleian Library*. In transliterating Yiddish names I have used the phonetic system, with regard, however, to the tradition prevailing in various European countries.

---

[1] Dr. Brawer, *op. cit.*, published only the last 40 pages of Ber's work. In his introductory remarks he refers to a couple of autobiographical notes in the *Dibré Binah*, which do not appear in the Memoirs.

[2] The thousands figure is commonly omitted in Hebrew (the so-called "short system"): thus 490 = 5490 A. M.

[3] For the calculation of the dates I have consulted Ed. Mahler, *Handbuch der Jüdischen Chronologie*, Leipzig, 1916.

Names like Hirsch and Schmeril are spelt in the German way. Names written in Latin characters — Polish, Hungarian, French and German — are given in the original spelling. For Russian and Ukrainian names I have made use of the phonetic transcription.

Titles of works in Hebrew, Polish and Russian quoted by me are as a rule translated into English in order to facilitate the printing. Works in Hebrew are marked (H.), works in Polish (P.), and works in Russian (R.). The titles of French, Latin and German books are given in their original wording.

It is my pleasant duty to record my appreciation of the help rendered me in my task. I am indebted to Dr. H. Hirschfeld, the Librarian of Jews' College, for kindly permitting me to copy the manuscript and supplying me with valuable information. My grateful acknowledgements are due to Dr. A. Büchler, Dr. M. Gaster and Dr. A. Marmorstein, who have made extremely important comments, and to Mr. Leon Simon, who has read the entire proofs and has made a number of improvements. Mr. A. P. Larke and Mr. T. B. Simmons have assisted me by reading the translation of the manuscript and making useful suggestions. Mr. Leveen, of the Oriental Department of the British Museum, has rendered me assistance on many occasions. I am also indebted to Dr. I. Feldman for having helped me in the interpretation of medical terms occurring in the manuscript. My thanks are due to my wife for her indefatigable and most valuable co-operation. I have, finally, to express my gratitude to all those who have rendered material support to this publication.

Oxford, August, 1922.

TABLE OF CONTENTS.

the leaseholder. — How Naḥman is the cause of the mishaps of the community. — The skill of the Jewish silversmiths and goldsmiths at Lemberg. — The Hungarian fireworeshipper. — On Parseeism and the origins of the Hungarian people. — Prideaux's book *Old and New Testament*. — The depreciation of Polish currency. — Bad Polish money. — Dissolution of the Council or *Vaad* of Four Lands. — New tax regulations. — Ber's appreciation of the work of the Council. — The census of Jewish taxpayers in Bolechow. — The meeting of Jewish Elders in Lemberg. — Ber's démarches on behalf of his native community. — The Confederation of Bar. — The first partition of Poland. — Ber's comment. — Bad times. — Lack of credit. — General uncertainty. — Impatient creditors. — The lease of the revenues of Bolechow. — Ber as leaseholder. — His failure. — Petitions to the landlord. — Ber recollects his early commercial experiences. — His acquaintance with Labadie. — Exchange of Hebrew and German lessons. — Labadie's scientific career. — He presents Ber with Prideaux's *Old and New Testament* in exchange for lambskins. — The subject of this book. — Dealings in wine. — Travels to Hungary and sales in Lemberg. — Transaction with Count Poniatowski, the Voyevoda of Kiew. — The Muscovite customer. — Ber tires of the partnership with his brother. — The jealous sister-in-law. — Dissolution of the partnership. — Ber concludes a new partnership.

APPENDIX.

Criticism of Prideaux's views on the coming of the Messiah. — The Polish priest, Jacob Radlinski. — Ber's rôle in the disputation with the Frankists. — The book of Giovanni Benesius Botero.

INTRODUCTION.

Among the records of the Court of the Voyevoda in Lemberg — the tribunal which in the days of the old Polish Republic heard lawsuits between Jews and Gentiles — there is a case brought against "Leyba and Berek, burgesses and tradesmen of Bolechow, and wine-merchants in Lemberg".[1] Leyba and Berek are proper names which tell us nothing; and this record would hardly have aroused interest had there not been discovered other documents, which throw light upon these persons. Leyba and Berek were two brothers, known to their contemporaries not only as tradesmen, but as prominent communal workers intimately associated with public affairs in Polish Jewry in the eighteenth century. The younger of them, Ber, or Berek, who in his later years assumed the family name of Birkenthal, wrote Memoirs, translated foreign books into Hebrew, and was the author of a work dealing with Jewish sectarian movements. In his Memoirs, as well as in his other writings, Ber often refers to his elder brother, Aryeh Loeb, a respected and able communal leader.

Ber's Memoirs throw a great deal of light on Jewish life in Eastern and Central Europe in the eighteenth century, an epoch so rich in problems and events. The French Revolution and the dismemberment of Poland were the outstanding events of that period, and both of them affected Jewry in the West and in the East. Ber was too old when the Revolution broke out to witness its results, but the wave of rationalism, which had been spreading from Western Europe as a forerunner of the

[1] Z. Pazdro, *The Organisation and Practice of the Voyevoda Court in the Period* 1740—1772 (P.), Lemberg. 1903, p. 35.

great political and social change, took hold of him and
many of his contemporaries. The ideology of the *Haskalah*[1]
found in Ber an early adherent. Towards the mystical
movements which had such influence among the Jewish
masses his attitude was that of a rather indulgent ob-
server; but he was ready to fight the aberrations of the
mystics when they menaced the foundations of Judaism.
The political changes which took place in Poland in his
days attracted his attention because they exerted a
decisive influence on the life and institutions of Polish
Jewry.

Before we discuss the subject-matter of Ber's Memoirs,
it is necessary to offer some observations on the environment in which the author of the Memoirs was brought up.

The town of Bolechow, in which Ber was born, is situated in Eastern Galicia, not far from the Carpathian
Mountains. Nicholas Giedsinski, the nobleman to whom
this property belonged, laid the foundations of the town
in 1612, and accorded it a charter, which defined the obligations and duties of all three nationalities living in Bolechow — Jews, Poles and Ruthenians — towards the
landlord. The Jews had settled before the place became
a town, but a regular community arose only after 1612,
when the charter granted by Giedsinski provided equal
rights and liberties for the Jews. They were allowed to
acquire landed property in the centre of the town and to
build houses there; a separate plot was ceded by the
landlord for the erection of a synagogue, together with
a plot of land on the other bank of the river which ran
through Bolechow, for use as a burial ground. There was no
ghetto at Bolechow, though most of the houses inhabited
by the Jews were situated close together. The Jews enjoyed the right of voting in the election of the burgomaster and the aldermen or councillors of the Municipal

---

[1] *Haskalah*, or enlightenment, an intellectual progressive movement
which arose among the Jews in Prussia in the middle of the eighteenth
century, chiefly under the leadership of Moses Mendelssohn, the philosopher
and translator of the Bible into German.

Council. The Municipal Court could not settle a cause between a Jew and a non-Jew without the assistance of representatives of the Jewish community. The newly-elected burgomaster had always to declare when taking the oath of office that he would safeguard and defend the rights of all three nationalities living at Bolechow. During the seventeenth century harmony prevailed in the relations between the Jews and their Gentile neighbours. The Jews enjoyed the confidence of the population, as may be gathered from the fact that they were entrusted with official commissions on behalf of the Municipal Council. The attitude of the landlords continued to be benevolent; thus, for example, in 1670, after the town was burned down and destroyed by the Tatars, the Jews were granted a loan by the landlords for the purpose of alleviating the position of their impoverished community.[1]

In our author's times conditions had undergone some change for the worse. Both in the policy of the administration and of the landlords, and in the attitude of the non-Jewish population, then were signs of malevolence and distrust, and even of open enmity. Nevertheless, Bolechow retained the features of the typical "private" estate, that is, a town belonging to a landlord and subject to his sovereignty and jurisdiction.[2] In these towns and townships the position of the Jews had always been in some way smoother than in the "royal towns", provided, naturally, that the landlords cared for the welfare of their estates and the people living thereon, and were not like those capricious and cruel tyrants described by Ber, by the philosopher Solomon Maimon[3], and by certain of the Polish memoir-writers.

---

[1] See *Allgemeine Zeitung des Judentums*, 1879, pp. 283—285 (extract from an article by N. Landes, *Aus der Geschichte der Juden in Bolechow*, in the Lemberg periodical *Der Israelit*).

[2] This was established by a law of the Polish Diet in 1538.

[3] *An Autobiography*, translated from the German by J. Clark Murray, London, 1888.

Bolechow was in those years known for its saltsprings [1], which provided a means of livelihood to Jewish lessees, sub-lessees and dealers. The Jews were also engaged in various branches of commerce, as, for instance, in wine, horses, cattle, etc. Bolechow was one of those innumerable towns in Poland, Lithuania and the Ukraine which owed their populousness and their vigorous life to their Jewish dealers and craftsmen. It was governed by the steward of the landlord, on whom in the least resort depended the safety and happiness of the population, and particularly of the Jews. Ber's account reveals the peculiarities of the life of his native town, the fears which filled his contemporaries when Bolechow changed its owner by inheritance or sale of the estate, the sorrows and anxiety caused by the arbitrary actions of despotic stewards, and also the few happy events which took place from time to time.

Ber's pedigree can be traced back to his great grandfather, Judah Loeb, whose son Hirsch was a native of the township of Meseritch (near Brest-Litowsk) and witnessed as a boy of eight the horrors which followed the rising of the Cossacks under the leadership of Khmelnitsky, in 1648. Nothing is on record of Hirsch's life, and we do not know how he came to establish himself at Bolechow. The Memoirs picture him as a venerable old man living there with his son Judah, Ber's father, and record his peaceful death in 1743.

Judah (born 1673) was a wine-merchant and innkeeper of considerable business capacity. He had more business interests than one — for instance, he was for a time engaged in farming estates — but his activities were mainly concentrated on the wine trade, which he brought to a high degree of development. He knew the Hungarian market, and enjoyed a well-deserved reputation among the wine-firms in that country. The experience which

---

[1] See *Geographical Dictionary of the Kingdom of Poland* (P.), s. v. Bolechow.

he gathered, in the course of his long and intimate connection with Hungarian business houses and wine-growers
among the nobility, greatly helped his sons, Aryeh Loeb
and Ber, in their commercial undertakings, the success
of which was due to the credit won by their father.
Judah was an amiable person, affable and communi-
cative. He had as great a command of the Polish and
Hungarian languages as of his native tongue, Yiddish,
and fascinated nobles and tradesmen alike by the proverbs
and stories which he told in all these languages. Owing to
his linguistic ability he was given an opportunity of acting
as interpreter between the Hungarian King Francis II.
Rakoczy and the Polish Hetman, Adam Nicholas Sieniawski. Judah was on good terms with the Polish nobles
and dignitaries, among whom was Count Stanislaus Poniatowski, the father of the last king, Stanislaus Augustus.
The elder Poniatowski was intimately and actively connected with diplomatic and military affairs from the
beginning of the eighteenth century, and Judah sometimes
learned from him what was happening in high politics.
Judah was thus a man of some experience in world affairs,
with an insight into the complicated international politics
of his time. He represented the type of Jew who did not
shut himself up in the narrow Jewish street, but took an
interest in general questions, and had his children taught
the Polish language so that they might have the same
breadth of interests. This was the mentality of Ber's father,
and the author of the Memoirs developed on similar lines.
Not very much is known of the author's mother, who
died when he was fourteen years old.

Ber was born at Bolechow on the 13th of March, 1723.
His elder brothers, Axelrod Bendet and Aryeh Loeb, were
both well known, the first as a Rabbinical scholar and the
second as a communal worker and merchant. A younger
brother, Zeeb Wolf, seems to have also become a tradesman. Ber had also a sister, Blimah. From his early youth
our author was given a religious education. Among his
teachers, some of whom he remembered by name, as

for example Elieser Liber and Joseph, special mention
must be made of the Chief Rabbi of Bolechow, Yukel
Segal Hurwitz, who was famous in his day, and was
honoured with a call to fill the post of Rabbi at Brody,
a centre of Jewish learning. Throughout his life our author
was influenced by his great teacher, and he kept in mind the
farewell address which the Rabbi delivered in the open
air before the whole assembled community when Ber was
eleven years old. The boy at that time witnessed great ex-
citement in his native town. The Polish State was disturbed
after the death of King Augustus II., when two candidates claimed the succession to the throne — the son
of the late king, Augustus, and Stanislaus Leszczyński.
France and Russia intervened, each supporting her favourite. Russian troops marched through Poland, repelling the
forces of Stanislaus Leszczyński. Various military detach-
mnts swept through Bolechow, and the town was in a state
of great agitation. The Rabbi was denounced to one of
the commanders as being in possession of great wealth,
and he had to flee on the eve of the Day of Atonement, an
event which made a lasting impression on Ber's young mind.

Ber's father, a man, as we have seen, of worldly
experience, was anxious to give his son a superior education. Our author studied Polish and Latin with no
common zeal and courage. In those days to keep a
Christian tutor for one's children was a thing unheard
of among Jews. A younger contemporary of Ber's, the
philosopher Solomon Maimon, tells of his own experience in that respect. "To learn Polish or Latin"
says Maimon, "with a Catholic teacher was for me impossible, on the one hand because the prejudices of my
own people prohibited to me all languages but Hebrew
and all sciences but the Talmud and the vast array of
its commentators, and on the other hand because the
prejudices of Catholics would not allow them to give
instruction on those matters to a Jew." [1] Ber, however,

---

[1] *Autobiography*, p. 89.

was brought up in more pleasant conditions. His father
was broadminded enough to tolerate and even to en-
courage the secular studies of his son, and a Christian
preceptor could be found who did not mind teaching
a Jewish boy.

Ber never touches on the more intimate side of his life,
but we may conjecture what the tragedy of his first marriage must have been. Imagine a youth inspired with high
hopes and proud ambitions, clever and studious, married
against his inclination to a mere child. "She proved not
the destined one" — these are the only words which Ber
utters concerning the failure of those two and a half
years during which he was chained to a wife who gave
him no children. His divorce apparently brought him
back his freedom and the opportunity of continuing his
beloved studies, which we may suppose him to have
neglected during that unhappy time. But then Ber was
faced with the hostile attitude of his countrymen. Both
his divorce and his linguistic accomplishments caused a
certain estrangement and mistrust among the Jewish
community of Bolechow. People began to talk of Ber's
attachment to non-Jewish subjects, and to suspect his
adherence to his ancestral faith. It was even said that
he would desert his religion. He therefore felt constrained to give up his Christian master and to abstain
from any but devotional pursuits.

This little drama of Ber, his intellectual fervour, his
family troubles, his illusions, his disappointment and re-
signation, would not perhaps interest us of itself, for it
tells the rather common story of the struggles of youth.
It acquires, however, particular significance when we
consider the time and the environment in which these
things happened. Ber was born about thirty years before
Maimon, and belonged to an older generation. For the
further understanding of the work of enlightenment carried
on some decades later by Moses Mendelssohn it is essential
to know what the generation of Ber was like, whether
there were already signs of that spiritual movement which

was to play such an important part in the cultural life of
Jewry. A characteristic feature of the Jewish revival
brought about by Mendelssohn was the idea of awaken-
ing to new life the Hebrew language. The Bible was
the basis of the work of Mendelssohn, the Biblical tongue
inspired him and his collaborators, the *Meassefim*,[1] and
a new epoch in Hebrew literature is closely connected
with that group. But before the watchword *Haskalah*,
which means Enlightenment, was crystallised and pro-
claimed, more or less successful attempts must have been
made in various Jewish quarters to revive the Hebrew
language, and to introduce science and general literature
among the Jewish people. We know of some precursors
of Mendelssohn, as, for instance, Aron Gompertz,[2] a physician and man of letters, and venture the hypothesis that
similar figures and tendencies were also to be met with in
Eastern Europe. Ber confirms this conjecture. He relates
how at Tysmienica, a town west of Stanislawow, where
he lived for a couple of years with his second wife in the
house of her father, he found congenial people, young
men with literary aspirations devoted to the study of
Hebrew. One of them, Joseph, son of Jacob Kopel, an
"admirable writer in the Holy Tongue" as Ber styles
him, left some literary works which Ber devotedly preserved after the death of his friend.[3]

In Bolechow, in Tysmienica, in Brody and in other towns
and townships of Eastern Galicia, we observe everywhere
in the first half of the eighteenth century symptoms of
a new movement, remarkable for its liberal-minded attitude towards general knowledge and for its devotion
to non-Rabbinical Hebrew literature. We stand at the
birth of a new epoch; we see the promoters of the

---

[1] A group of authors, who wrote for the first Hebrew literary monthly
Ha-Meassef.

[2] See D. Kaufmann, *Die Familie Gompertz*, where particulars of this
personality are given.

[3] Nothing is known to-day of this writer. Ber, unfortunately, lost some
of his books during a fire which occurred at Bolechow, in 1759.

Haskalah movement at work, long before Mendelssohn, paving the way. for his ideas, preparing the ground for his supporters. But these early pioneers of the *Haskalah*, the contemporaries of Ber, did not transcend the bounds of the old tradition. They wore the old-fashioned dress, and did not differ in their religious life and practices from their Jewish environment.

Later on, in the first half of the nineteenth century, Eastern Galicia became one of the centres of the new progressive movement in Jewry, a movement which produced such men as the philosopher Nachman Krochmal, the critic S. L. Rappaport, the educationalist Joseph Perl, the satirist I. Erter, and many other gifted authors who gathered round them circles of admirers and followers. Books and periodicals appeared which will ever retain their value. The scope of education was widened and deepened at the same time. The Eastern Galician *Haskalah* covers a brilliant page in the history of Jewish spiritual life.[1] This movement cannot be understood without reference to the aspirations which we find some hundred years earlier in Ber's days. When considering that early stage of the development of *Haskalah* we have to remember that Tysmienica, Brody, Bolechow, Lemberg etc., were in close touch with foreign commercial centres. The Jewish merchants of Tysmienica had business relations with Breslau; those of Brody went all over the Continent, and played a considerable part in the subsequent stages of the new educational movement. The needs of commercial intercourse made this change imperative. The trading section of the Jewish population could not shut itself up within the narrow limits of a purely religious education. They came to realise that they must widen their spiritual horizon by acquiring general knowledge, by learning the languages spoken by the neighbouring nations, and by attaching themselves to European culture.

[1] Max Weissberg, *Die Neuhebräische Aufklärungsliteratur in Galizien*, 1898.

Ber, however, did not belong to those heated
imaginations who would have liked to abolish all traditional education whatever. If in his youth he may have
criticised mere Talmudic book-learning, we see that in
later years, when he wrote his reminiscences, he spoke
of the scholastic and hair-splitting method called *Pilpul*,
in which he had been brought up, without resentment
or irony. So he recalls how "at first the Rabbi himself stood up and expounded with all his profound
knowledge and great subtlety the novelties he had discovered in the legal discussions of the Talmud"; how
"afterwards the students and pupils all propounded their
ideas by this hair-splitting method".[1] This consisted in
inventing novelties by cunning combinations *(Chiddushim)*.
The brain of the student laboured to extort ever
new meanings from the Talmud and its interpreters. Ber
went through this school of subtle argument, which
has long been the characteristic feature of Talmudic
learning in Poland. At Tysmienica he had an opportunity
of perfecting himself in the Talmudic discipline under the
guidance of R. Isaac, who afterwards occupied the Rabbinical chair at Gwosdziec, and of R. Monish,[2] the Rabbi
of the community at Tysmienica. He also came in contact
with other learned men, thanks to whom he widened his
Rabbinic knowledge. Moreover, he came there under
the influence of the *Cabbala*, the secret teaching. One
day the book of the pseudo-Messiah Shabbetai Zebi's
"prophet" Nathan Ghazzati, entitled *Hemdat Yamim*,
reached the *Beth-ha-Midrash* (House of Study) of Tysmienica. This cabbalistic prayer-book, containing also
hints for cabbalistic practices and morals, and finally
dealing with the transmigration of souls and the raising
of spirits, caused a great ferment among the students.
They took to invoking spirits, practised self-castigation,

---

[1] This is one of the few autobiographical references in Ber's work
Dibre Binah, which has been published in part by Dr. A. Brawer, in
Hashiloah, vol. 33. pp. 150, *sq.*

[2] Brawer, *ibid.*, p. 152.

beat their chests with stones, and threw themselves on the ground before the synagogues during the reading of the Law. Ber was among these revivalists and fervent adepts of cabbalistic practices, which obsessed the people at Tysmienica. "It seems", he writes, "that it was impossible for anybody to bear such deadly blows as those which I gave myself in my youth".[1]

The country on both sides of the Carpathian Mountains, in which Ber and his relatives lived and moved, was in those days crammed with sectarians, the adherents of Shabbetai Zebi. The towns of Nadworna and Maramaros-Sziget in particular had been Shabbetaian centres for decades. Ber was acquainted with some of these sectarians, who happened to stay at his father's inn.[2]

After his second marriage, which was a happy one, Ber, being then twenty years old, took to commerce, which occupation did not, however, detach him from his scholarly pursuits. On the contrary, in his hours of leisure he continued his studies in the various fields into which they had been directed in his early youth. Hebrew literature occupied the first place in his mind — the Talmud, the Zohar, the mediaeval philosophers and moralists and, finally, contemporary authors. Ber was fond of rare and valuable books, which he used to collect with great zeal. He also continued the study of foreign languages. Besides Polish and Latin, he devoted himself to French and to German,[3] which latter language he studied not only for commercial purposes, but with a view to being able to assimilate its literature and to acquire erudition in various branches of knowledge. He had a particular taste for the humanities — history, theology and polemical and apologetic literature. A survey of the works which Ber read and eventually tried to render into Hebrew is valuable for his biographers, as it shows what intelligent Jews used

[1] *Ibid.*, p. 152.
[2] *Ibid.*, p. 331.
[3] Concerning French see Brawer, *ibid.*, p. 151. The occasion on which Ber took up the study of German is described in detail in the Memoirs.

to read in those days. Ber was in this respect by no
means an exception, for there were certainly others who
had a similar inclination for literature and science outside
the range of Hebrew learning.

Naturally enough, our author's mind, trained in
Biblical and Talmudic studies, was particularly attracted
by books on geography and history dealing with countries and populations of the Orient, and in many ways
connected with the Jewish past. The time for critical
research and archeological evidence had not yet come;
the books which we are now to mention were based on
literary tradition. Take, for example, the once famous
book *Relazioni Universali* of the Italian historian and
geographer Giovanni Benesius Botero, which had a wide
circulation throughout Europe.[1] This work, giving a
description of the history, the customs, the character
and the natural riches of divers nations and countries,
could not fail deeply to interest Ber, and he undertook
to translate several parts of it into Hebrew.[2] Some
portions of this translation deal with the Abyssinians,
who according to Botero "had accepted Judaism from
Melech, the son of King Solomon and the Queen of
Sheba"[3]; and it may be assumed that Ber was guided
in his choice by a particular interest in the subject.

Ber was also deeply engrossed in the study of
Humphrey Prideaux's work *The Old and New Testament
connected in the History of the Jews and the neighbouring
Nations from the declension of the Kingdom of Israel
and Judah to the time of Christ.*[4] He became acquainted

---

[1] First edition 1592—1595. Three editions appeared in Poland, the first in
1609, the second in 1613 and the third, under a somewhat altered title, *Teatrum
Świata wszystkiego* (Theatre of the Whole World) in 1659. See *Encyklopedya
Powszechna*, vol. IV. As we have already noted in our preface, a copy of the
last edition of this work was presented to Ber by a Polish noble in 1759.

[2] They are included in the manuscript at Jews' College, London.

[3] See third Polish edition, part IV. book 3, p. 218.

[4] London, 1716—1718. Very frequently reprinted. "Though now", says
the Dictionary of National Biography, "out of date, it supplied for a long
time a real want and stimulated further study".

with this publication in a German version, and attempted to make a Hebrew translation of it; but his endeavour to publish in that tongue the work of the Oxford writer, "which", Ber said, "would be of great enlightenment to our Jewish scholars", was not successful. However, the several pages preserved in the Jews' College copy afford another proof of his literary activities. The Hebrew adaptation of Botero and Prideaux would, if published, have served the development of Hebrew by the interpretation of the various historical, geographical, ethnographical and literary matters treated in those works. Ber's efforts in this direction are of importance for two reasons. He became intimate with Western European scholarship, and he learned to write a concise, scientific and fluent Hebrew, free from the flowery figures of speech so often to be met with in the Jewish authors of the eighteenth century.

Ber appears to have been acquainted with the writings of Josephus and the patristic literature, which latter he may have known not at first hand, but through the various theological works of which he was an assiduous reader.[1] He seems to have specialised in Polish books and pamphlets written with the purpose of attacking the principles of Judaism. This kind of literature was abundant in the eighteenth century, particularly that dealing with the sectarian movement of the Frankists. Our author made it his business to read newly-published books on these subjects as well as the older literature.[2] His extensive reading is well illustrated by some of his quotations from Hugo Grotius,[3] from Gregorio Leti's *Treatise on Italy*,[4] from the *Foundations of General History* by the German

---

[1] See *Hashiloaḥ*, vol. 33, p. 151.

[2] Jacob Radlinski, *Prawda chrzescijańska, to jest list Rabina Samuela do Rabina Izaka*, etc., Lublin, 1732; Gaudenty Pikulski, *Złość Żydowska*, 1760, and several other books and pamphlets.

[3] See Brawer, *Hashiloaḥ*, vol. 38. p. 351.

[4] *L'Italia regnante o vera nuova descriptione dello stato presente . . d'Italia*, Genoa 1675. See Brawer, vol. 38. p. 352.

scholar J. H. Zopf,[1] from R. F. Bellarmine's treatise *De Verbo Dei*,[2] and so on. When we add the great knowledge of history, theology and philosophy, and of the cabbala and sectarian movements, which he acquired in Hebrew, we cannot but admire the erudition of this man, who after all, being a business man, could only spare a little time for intellectual pursuits.

Ber's activities in the field of commerce lead us into the economic and social life of Polish Jewry in the eighteenth century, to which we must now give some attention.

The area in which Ber lived and worked was in former centuries designated "Red Ruthenia", or the province of Rus, and is to-day called Eastern Galicia or Western Ukraine. It is a fertile country, and abounds in natural wealth. The Jews appeared here as far back as the fourteenth century, if not earlier. In time they developed in numerical strength and in significance for the economic life of the country. In the sixteenth century they formed about 5 per cent of the whole of the inhabitants, and about 20 per cent of the urban population. They were occupied in rural colonisation, in commerce, in moneylending, in leasing public revenues, in the exploitation of the mineral deposits, such as salt, and in various trades. Lemberg, the capital and chief commercial city of the province, where the trade routes from Turkey, Moldavia and Hungary to the West and North-West converged, was the seat of the largest Jewish community, which passed through a prosperous stage of development at the close of the sixteenth and the beginning of the seventeenth century. Wholesale commerce then occupied a high place among both the non-Jewish and the Jewish trading classes. The Jews were engaged chiefly in Oriental commerce, for which Lemberg has always been a connecting link, and in dealing in cattle, timber, grain and wine.

[1] *Erlaeuterte Grundlegung der Universal-Historie bis zum Jahre 1773*, 17th ed. Halle. 1779.
[2] See Brawer, vol. 38. p. 352.

In the seventeenth century affairs assumed a more sombre aspect. The economic activities of the Jews underwent considerable restrictions. The nobility had managed to monopolise the grain trade; others, including Jews, could engage in that trade only at the behest or in the service of the nobles. Moreover, the Christian merchants and craftsmen contrived to meet the competition of the Jews by prohibiting or restricting their participation in certain branches of commerce and manual callings. Disputes and struggles ensued, as a consequence of which the position of the Jewish dealer and artisan was weakened. In the middle of that century Poland was handicapped by the rising of the Cossacks, foreign invasion and civil war. The Polish State became insecure. Economic conditions grew worse, and the Jews were naturally affected by the economic collapse. The bulk of the people became impoverished.

In the eighteenth century conditions took a further turn for the worse. The general uncertainty of things, the chronic state of anarchy and lawlessness, the decline of the authority of the Crown, the weakening of the very foundations of the state, its final disruption — all this kept the Jews in a constant condition of insecurity and anxiety. In any survey of this process of decomposition the far-reaching results of the disastrous invasions of Poland by the Cossacks, Tatars, Muscovites, Swedes and Turks in the seventeenth century must be taken into account. These invasions brought in their train untold misery, wholesale destruction and pestilence. The country would have needed at least several decades of peace and a strong and wise government to put it on its legs again. But neither was John Sobieski fitted for this task, nor was Poland to enjoy the peace which was indispensable to its recovery. The Northern War broke out, and the country was for years again ravaged and ruined by foreign troops. New wounds were added to those which had not yet healed. The once powerful and rich land had become a puppet in the hands of the neighbouring states, which grew

mighty and prosperous at the expense of Poland. Sweden
barred the way to the Baltic by conquering Livonia.
During the Saxon period, which lasted for nearly seventy
years, the Polish state ceased to play an active part in
international politics; it was made instead an object of
international diplomatic intrigues. Foreign ambassadors
practically assumed control of the country; foreign armies
marched up and down the land, disregarding the right of
Polish sovereignty. In times of interregnum the complete
disintegration of the nation became particularly apparent;
the constant bickering of the political factions led to more
serious dissensions, and civil strife and domestic fury con-
vulsed the state. The nobility, headed by the magnates,
both spiritual and temporal, formed two hostile camps,
which waged war on one another with the moral and
·material support of Russia or France or any other foreign
power. These internal troubles shook the Polish Common-
wealth to its very foundations.

Polish publicists and memoirists who happened to live and
to play their part in those unfortunate years pictured the
break-down of their native land and the approaching exhaus-
tion of the nation. But as they were mostly themselves concerned in that fratricidal strife, they were of course biassed
when they enlarged on the merits of their own leaders and
condemned the policy of their adversaries. We should,
therefore, welcome the evidence of an impartial eye-
witness, of an outsider, who merely observed the trend
of events. Ber was such an outsider. As a Jew he could
not of course dream of taking any share in the political life of the country. What he knew of the turbu-
lent course of contemporary politics was based either
on personal observation, or on information from various
channels, sometimes from the chief actors in the drama themselves. He also learned much from his father
Judah, and he in turn had received his information from high
dignitaries, who stood at the very cradle of political
developments. Moreover, Ber was, as we know, fond of
reading historical books, the contents of which he combined

with knowledge obtained from other sources. On one
occasion he says that he obtained his information from
Polish chronicles.

The Memoirs include several paragraphs touching upon
some interesting episodes of eighteenth century Polish
history. In most of the cases the author's observations
are short but to the point. Thus, for instance, Ber makes
the following remark with regard to the Confederation
of Bar, that originally genuine popular rising against
King Stanislaus Augustus and the Senate in the years
1768—1772: "There was no law or court of law in the
Polish country. Might was superior to right." He had
naturally in mind the great chaos into which Poland
was then plunged. A younger contemporary of his, the
poet Francis Karpinski, pictured in a similar way the
anarchy provoked by this uprising.[1] Students of those
momentous events which ultimately led to the first partition of Poland — an outcome also foreshadowed in the
Memoirs — might find in our author's account some new
items of interest, worthy of a place in this variegated
historical picture. We watch with our author how one of
the leading personalities of the Confederation, Count
Joachim Potocki, secludes himself in his castle at Trembowla for a whole winter in order to compose procla-
mations to be sent out to all the Polish nobles, appealing
to them to join the imminent rising. We listen to the same
Potocki when he warns Ber against carrying his wines to
Lemberg in view of the coming troubles and insecurity,
because he in his capacity as landlord of the town of
Bolechow would be unable to protect his townfolk from
robbery. Thus our author knew some time before the
outbreak of the Confederation that troublesome days
would ensue. Later on, when the revolt was in full swing
and France interfered on behalf of the Confederates, Ber
followed carefully the trend of events. A French emissary,

*Count
Joachim
Potocki*

---

[1] See his *Memoirs* (P.) with an introduction by Peter Chmielowski,
Warsaw, 1898, p. 40.

who carried 200.000 ducats from his Government for the support of the Confederation, stayed with Ber, who consequently learned about the Frenchman's mission. On the other hand, Ber tells us that King Stanislaus Augustus had asked the Russian Government for an expeditionary corps of 24,000 men to be sent for the purpose of suppressing the rising. How far this and other similar information is really in accordance with the facts is a matter for further examination.

The Memoirs also throw some side lights on the period of the Saxon dynasty, with special reference to Count Stanislaus Poniatowski, the father of the last Polish King, and one of the central political figures of that time. The opinion of the historians as to the character and rôle of Poniatowski in eighteenth century Polish history is divided. Whilst his biographer Kantecki praises him highly as a statesman, one of the ablest Polish historians, Professor Askenazy, styles Poniatowski "a daring and successful condottiere".[1] In our author's pen-picture Poniatowski appears as a shrewd politician, who perfectly understands how to handle King Augustus II and the nobility, becomes the King's favourite after having ardently fought in the front ranks of his enemies, succeeds in getting several high Governmental offices into his hands, and knows how to rule the gentry at their local Diets, or Seyms, by means of his persuasive speech, by bribing them with all sorts of valuable little presents, and, above all, by lavishly entertaining them with wine.

The stormy years which followed the death of King Augustus II (1733) have been treated by Polish historians from many aspects; but they have neglected the episode of the invasion by Russian troops from the Ukraine of the neighbouring Polish provinces of Podolia and Red Ruthenia. Ber's impressive story of the anxious days through which his native place and other towns in these

---

[1] K. Kantecki, *Stanislaus Poniatowski*, (P), Posen 1880; Szymon Askenazy, *Two Centuries* (P), vol. I (1901), p. 204.

districts passed in the course of this military advance provides some local material for the study of that period.

We realise once more, in reading this passage, how fast and irretrievably Poland was marching towards its ruin. Sensible politicians raised their voices in appeals to the patriotism, honesty and reason of their fellow-citizens. They failed, however, for the public spirit of the country was at its lowest. The symptons of the evil which had eaten into the whole governmental machinery became evident in the disintegration of both the legislature and the executive. The Diets of the time of the Saxon dynasty could but very seldom cope with their programme, for they were in most cases crippled by the application of the *liberum veto*, which meant that no resolution of the Diet could be valid unless adopted unanimously by all the members. Even one single member who disliked a pro- posed law was able to suspend the proceedings by ex- claiming "I disapprove". The exercise of the *liberum veto* became a regular feature of the Polish constitutional practice of that time; in effect it uprooted the constitution and destroyed its life. Side by side with this degeneration of the legislature, the defects of the administrative appa- ratus assumed ever larger and more threatening dimensions. A saying became current: "Poland exists by disorder."[1] The peasantry was enslaved, and the towns were deprived of political rights. All political influence and social power were vested in two comparatively small sections of the nation, the nobility, or *szlachta*, and the clergy.

The nobility, having attained in the course of years the maximum of rights and immunities, was content to enjoy its superior position, while refusing any obligations towards the State. The nobles cared nothing for the

[1] Coined by the satirist Opalinski. See Linde, *Dictionary of the Polish language* (P.), vol. 3. The growing anarchy in Poland in the eighteenth century has been treated by various authors. The general outlines are given in the following works: Lewinski-Korwin, *Political History of Poland*, New York: 1917, pp. 276. *sq.* R. Nisbet Bain, *Slavonic Europe*, Chapter VIII, 1908; R. Roepell, *Polen um die Mitte des XVIII. Jahrhunderts*, 1876.

welfare of the country, but only for their own happiness
and comfort. "The long-sought political Utopia of the
szlachta had, in fact, at last been realised; they lived in
a land where every gentleman had nothing to do but to
please himself."[1] Ber's reminiscences abound in references
to the gay and secure life of the *szlachta* in the days of
Augustus III (1733—1763), when the easy-going temper
of the Polish nobles was at its best.

From his earliest youth every member of the Polish
nobility — including the middle-class gentleman and the
poor squire who lived as a retainer at the court of his
noble and powerful brother — was brought up with the
idea that he was the supreme person in the state, free
and unhampered by any law or authority. Within his
estate (and several estates covered thousands of square
miles, including towns, townships and villages), the noble
was *the* ruler. This might be either good or bad for the
population of these vast areas, for side by side with
reasonable, enlightened and humane magnates, there were
tyrannical and capricious landlords, who made the life of
the population subject to their jurisdiction a real hell.
Literature has preserved some vivid portraits of Polish
landlords of the bad type, like Count Nicholas Potocki,
the Starosta[2] of Kaniow, and Prince Radziwill, one of
the foremost grandees of Lithuania, in the writings of
the poet Niemcewicz and the philosopher Maimon, and
also in the Chronicle of Lemberg.[3] The present Memoirs
add a couple of specimens to this collection — Prince
John Kajetan Jablonowski and Prince Martin Lubomirski.
Of Lubomirski we learn that he indulged in brigandage
on the highways, robbing passing merchants and even
killing them. The merchant who carried Polish raw stuffs
to the marts at Breslau, Leipzig and Frankfurt (on the

---

[1] R. Nisbet Bain, *Slavonic Europe*, p. 380.

[2] Head of the local administration.

[3] J. U. Niemcewicz, *Memoirs* (P.), 1848, p. 82; S. Maimon, *An Autobiography*, p. 81 *sq.*. Zubrzycki, *The Chronicle of the Town of Lemberg*,
(P.), 1844, p. 478.

Oder), and brought back manufactured goods, was thus
exposed to the whim of a filibustering nobleman. The
position of the shopkeeper was no less precarious. A report
on Poland's commerce drawn up by careful Austrian
officials, who made a special business tour through that
country in 1756, says: "The Polish nobleman often comes
to a shop, asks for some stuff and orders the shopkeeper
to cut what he needs. Then he takes the stuff and fixes
the terms of payment. The shopkeeper has to accept his
price; otherwise he may consider himself lucky if he
receives back the cut stuff, for in most cases the nobleman
simply carries away the material and heaps insults on the
dealer, declares the dealer's mistrust of him to be an
offence to his noble status, and even threatens to draw his
sword. The frightened shopkeeper has to smooth his
furious customer down by all manner of submissiveness."[1]
Such statements, originating from unprejudiced foreigners,
confirm the correctness of Ber's records. Ber did not
blame for the sake of blaming. He liked rather to state
facts, and if the facts showed that among the nobility there
were real gentlemen, who behaved correctly to people
not of their own class, these facts were related by him
with the same impartiality and objectiveness. Sympathy
is expressed with such representatives of the Polish
nobility as Countess J. Wielhorska, Princess Lubomirska,
Count Stanislaus Poniatowski, Count Joachim Potocki,
the Grand Hetman Count Joseph Potocki, the ecclesiastic
Wieniawski, and others. Ber shows warm appreciation
of the interest exhibited by a group of landlords in the
neighbourhood of Bolechow in the fate of the Jewish
community after a terrible conflagration in 1759. The
relations between the gentry and the Jewish population
are depicted here in their more friendly aspect; the rough-
ness is somewhat softened.

[1] See A. Fournier, *Handel und Verkehr in Ungarn und Polen um die
Mitte des XVIII. Jahrhunderts*, in *Archiv für Österreichische Geschichte*,
vol. LXIX (1887), p. 440.

Clergy

Next to the nobility, the clergy exercised a very great influence in public affairs. The members of the ecclesiastical hierarchy were mostly recruited from the prominent families of the nobility. The clergy was entrusted with the education of the young. Enlightened Polish writers have pointed to the sinister rôle played by the clergy, both priests and monks, in moulding the minds of the young generations of the gentry. The clergy, which grew ever more powerful, and covered the country with an enormous number of monasteries and churches, seemed to have made it its special business to imbue the Polish nation with insidious hatred against the non-Catholic sections of the population, the Lutherans, Jews and Greek Orthodox alike. Poland became a bigoted, intolerant country. Such is the opinion of a very deep student of that time, M. Wladislaus Smolenski. He has come to the conclusion that the spiritual leaders of the country during the Saxon period, instead of taking part in the intellectual movement of the West, kept the people in ignorance.[1] Our Jewish memoirist, who was on friendly terms with prominent members of the cathedral chapter of Lemberg, does not condemn the clergy in so wholesale a fashion. He complains only of the anti-Semitic literature which was concocted in some ecclesiastical circles, a literature of which he made a special study, and which appeared to him a tissue of lies and stupidity.[2] He regretted these malicious attacks on Judaism, and could not refrain from expressing his indignation at them. Unfortunately this propaganda bore fruit. It became a custom of the students of the Catholic Colleges to amuse themselves by falling upon Jewish shops and dwellings, plundering them and beating their inhabitants. These barbarous outbursts were known in the annals of the Jewish communities as "The Scholars' Attacks" (*Schiler-*

[1] See the quotations from his work in Lewinski-Korwin. *op. cit.* p. 290—291.

[2] A younger contemporary of Ber, Solomon Bennet, who lived in the north of the Polish State, expresses his horror at the propaganda of the clergy. See his remarkable book, *The Constancy of Israel*, 1809, London, p. 215.

geloif). Ber witnessed what he calls the "last" atttack at Lemberg, in 1751.

The period of economic prosperity had gone, after having reached its climax in the sixteenth and the first half of the seventeenth century. It was then that Danzig and the other Baltic ports, which after the incorporation of Prussia and Livonia were controlled by Poland, acquired their importance for the Polish grain trade.[1] While timber and potash were also carried along the Vistula to Danzig, grain and cereals remained the staple commodities. In 1648 there were brought to Danzig 300,000 tons of grain, the highest figure ever noted in Polish times. After that year, however, things changed radically. The political disintegration, to which we have already alluded, had its economic effects. The conquest of Livonia by Sweden dealt a heavy blow at Polish commerce. Meanwhile the Dutch had established direct relations with Archangel, and as a result Russian grain began to play a significant part in the supply of Western Europe. Finally, agriculture having made some progress in France and England during the seventeenth century, Polish grain was in less demand than in earlier times. This general tendency would itself have sufficed to impair the economic prospects of Poland; and foreign invasions and constant civil war made the ruin complete. The export of grain from Danzig fell in 1715 to about 7,000 tons, and in 1737 as low as 4,782 tons. Polish money depreciated in value. A new *zlot* or gulden was coined, called *Tynf*, which contained only two-fifths of silver and three-fifths of copper. Foreign currency accordingly rose in price; the ducat went up from 6 Polish gulden to 12, the thaler from 3 to 6. This naturally affected foreign trade, and particularly the import of goods into Poland. The once famous marts, like Cracow, Lemberg

[1] The following survey of the economic conditions of Poland from the sixteenth till the beginning of the eighteenth century is chiefly based on M. A. Szelągowski. *The Economic and Social Development of Poland till 1795* (P.), in vol. II of the collection entitled "*Polska. Obrazy i opisy*" (Lemberg, 1909), pp. 666—672.

and Lublin, became "phantoms of their former selves."
As a modern English author has said,[1] they sank to the
level of vegetating provincial towns. Sieges, epidemics and
conflagrations finally ruined the old cities. The population
decreased, and half of the arable land remained un-
cultivated.[2]

Towards the middle of the eighteenth century some
brighter spots appeared on the dark horizon. The reign
of Augustus III was on the whole a period of stagnation,
but at least it was undisturbed by wars. Things began to
quieten down, and the trading class felt more at ease.
If the old cities had decayed, new towns belonging to
private owners, like Brody, Berdyczew, Dubno, Stanislawow, Tyśmienica and others, commenced to develop
trade, and reached a certain degree of prosperity. These
developments, minor, perhaps, but still not negligible, have
not yet been fully followed out by Polish historians,
because of the scantiness of the sources. The present
Memoirs afford priceless information on this subject.
We come at once to realise that there was not a complete
deadlock, that on the by-ways of Polish life there was
still some movement.

But even as regards the general commercial position,
the estimate of modern Polish authors needs some modi-
fication. In the perspective of history things are apt to
take on a gloomy aspect. A contemporary traveller, the
Austrian manufacturer Procop, held a rather hopeful view
as to the condition of trade in the Polish towns in the
fifties of the eighteenth century.[3] He records the fact
that consignments of timber, grain and potash were
brought to and exported from Danzig, and that cattle,
skins, tallow, wax and salt were brought to Breslau and
Frankfurt (on the Oder), where they were exchanged for
cloth, linen and woollen stuffs, drugs, gold and silver

---

[1] R. Nisbet Bain, *The last King of Poland and his Contemporaries*,
1909, p. 40.

[2] A. Szelągowski, *op. cit.* pp. 671—672.

[3] See A. Fournier, *op. cit.* p. 370, 446.

articles, fancy goods, Nuremberg wares, and so on. These statements may be completed from the more detailed records of Ber, who refers also to trade relations with Saxony and Hungary. The map in this volume shows the places which the author visited himself, or which are mentioned in connection with the commercial activities of his contemporaries. The routes which he used when he travelled to Hungary are also marked on the map.

The town of Lemberg still had its Fairs, at which, in addition to the ordinary business, the nobles used to sell or mortgage their properties, and to contract and repay debts. In Ber's time the wine trade appears to have been important, but from all that we gather from the Memoirs there was no great activity in other branches of commerce. Our author is more eloquent when he speaks of the rising star east of Lemberg, the town of Brody. He tells a striking story of how the Jewish traders there attained an exceptional position in international commerce, thanks to a considerable loan advanced to them by the landlord of the town, and to their own spirit of enterprise. Light is thrown on a place called Tysmienica, to-day a poor township in Galicia, but in those years renowned for its Armenian and Jewish merchants. Of the latter we hear that they had brisk commercial relations with Breslau. But the fullest and most important information is to be gathered concerning the Hungarian towns and villages situated in the mountainous Hegyalia region, famous for its wine, which is called Tokay after the chief place of that district. Students of the history of the Hungarian wine trade will learn much from Ber's exhaustive records and detailed figures concerning quantities of production, qualities, prices, conditions of payment, transport etc. He knew Tokay as if it were his native place; every trader, every wine-cellar, every shop there was familiar to him.

The real importance of the Memoirs, however, lies in the extremely valuable information which they give with regard to organisation of trade, rules of business, customs,

commercial intercourse, conditions of coinage and currency, credit and prices. It would lead us far beyond the
scope of these few introductory remarks if we were to
examine each of these subjects. It must suffice to touch
on those points of which the elucidation is indispensable
to a comprehensive understanding of the Memoirs.

Polish coinage in the eighteenth century was in a rather
confused and unsettled state, and according to Ber this
seriously affected trade. The lowest denomination of the
Polish monetary system was the *chelong*. Three *chelongs*
made a *grosz* or gross; thirty *grosz* made a *zlot*, or Polish
gulden, or florin (about 6 d.) Foreign currencies rose in
price in the first half of the eighteenth century. The ducat,
for instance, went up to 16 or even 18 gulden, and the thaler
to 8 gulden. New coins had not been minted for a long
time. Instead the country was glutted with coins minted
abroad, in Saxony and Prussia. Very soon after the outbreak of the Seven Years' War debased coins made their
appearance, largely imported from those countries. The
finances of the Prussian King Frederick II having become
precarious, he took to issuing depreciated money. The
Prussian masters of the mint began also to coin Polish
gulden with the image and superscription of the King
of Poland, and these were of a very low standard. The
intrinsic value of the coinage fell continuously; thus, for
instance, in 1758 18 thaler were coined from the mark of
fine silver, in 1759 30 thaler, and in 1762 40 thaler, whereas
the proper standard was 14 thaler only.[1] Our author vividly
pictures this process. We learn from him what is not
brought out by other memoir-writers of that time,[2] that
the money paid in by the Polish merchants, who regularly
visited Breslau and Frankfurt (on the Oder), was collected
by the masters of the mint, who then broke up these coins

[1] See Max Kirmiss, *Einleitung in die polnische Münzkunde*, in *Zeitschrift
der Geschichte für die Provinz Posen*, vol. *VI*; C. Grünhagen, *Schlesien unter
Friedrich dem Großen*, Breslau, *1890*, vol. *II, p. 126;* Schrötter and Schmoller,
Das preußische Münzwesen im XVIII. Jahrhundert, vol. *III*. See Index.

[2] So, for instance, A. Kitowicz, *Memoirs* (P.) vol. I, p. 48, *sq.*

and minted new ones of an inferior standard. The new coins were so poor in silver that they represented a value of only $7^1/_2$ or even 5 kreuzer, whilst the gulden received from the Polish tradesmen equalled 19 kreuzer. A whole series of these debased coins came into circulation, altogether a dozen varieties, such as *Bonki*, *Berlinki*, *Ephraimitki* and so forth. In 1760 there appeared in Warsaw a gulden almost wholly of iron, which was worth only 7 *grosz*. Suspicion was aroused that this coin also was of Prussian origin,[1] and public opinion was greatly stirred. Meanwhile more and more of the debased money streamed into the country, and these grossly depreciated coins drove out the good, heavy silver pieces. The exchangers reaped the advantage, and people of all classes took to this profitable occupation — noblemen, Jewish money-brokers and Catholic priests[2]; but the general public and the traders suffered severely and became very alarmed. Confusion grew ever greater. Fóreign currency at once rose: ducats, for instance, were bought at 23, 27 and even 28 gulden. This depreciation was accompanied by a rise in prices. Our author laments that all goods became dearer. Wine rose in price, and flour went up to twice the normal. Money lost all its value. So Ber preferred to give his wine on credit in the hope of better times to come. In the same way his creditors of the nobility did not care to accept payment of their debts, "for", says Ber, "they had learned that a new standard was going to be fixed for the gulden."

The State Treasurer Theodore Wessel in fact issued, on the 12th of August 1761, an ordinance in accordance with which all gulden coming from foreign mints were to be reduced in value — viz., the Saxon to 36 *grosz* and those coined in Prussian mints to 15 *grosz*. This was a reduction to less than half the previous standard.[3] The

---

[1] Schrötter and Schmoller, *op. cit.* vol. III, p. 58.

[2] Wladislaus Konopczynski, *Poland in the Epoch of the Seven Years' War*, (P.) part II, p. 176, *sq.*

[3] Besides the various authorities quoted in the previous notes, see J. Zagorski, *The coins of Old Poland*, 1845, (P.), pp. 171—176.

ordinance, however, remained wholly inoperative. The
ordinary man in the street could not distinguish the right
coin from the debased one. A. Kitowicz, the memoirist,
says that for a certain time the circulation of money ceased
throughout the country. Creditors refused to accept payment of debts unless it was made in currency of the new
standard, while on the other hand debtors were not willing
to pay otherwise than in the old currency, and this led
to innumerable disputes. Good silver money disappeared.
By another ordinance issued in the same year the value
of the gulden minted in Prussia was fixed at 25 *grosz* and
one *chelong*. Was this step taken by the State Treasurer
in recognition of the 100,000 Rhenish thaler which he had
received as a bribe from the King of Prussia?[1] A new
ordinance followed in 1762, in which again the standard
of the Breslau gulden was set partly at 15 and partly at
25 *grosz*. But all these enactments remained ineffective,
and the depreciated coins continued to circulate in the
country. In such circumstances Ber's trade operations
became less profitable, and we find him towards the sixties
of the eighteenth century in financial difficulties and in
trouble with his creditors. This leads us to the question
of credit, with special reference to the Jews.

In the early period of their history in Poland the Jews
were to a considerable extent engaged in money-lending,
for, being then almost the only trading community in the
country, they had the liquid assets which were necessary
to the king, the nobles and the burgesses. In time, however,
a non-Jewish trading element grew up, and the nobles,
after securing the monopoly of the grain trade, as we
have mentioned in another connection, became a wealthy
class. Simultaneously the Church was enriched by donations,
and, as in Western Europe, the monasteries and cathedral
chapters developed into big financial institutions. The Jewish
economic position, on the contrary, deteriorated. This decline

---

[1] See Schrötter and Schmoller, *op. cit.* vol. III, pp. 58 *sq.* and documents
NN. 42, 43 & 46.

was precipitated by a stubborn and merciless struggle
with the Christian tradesmen, a struggle which lasted
for centuries and enfeebled both the parties. The position
of the Jews was worsened still further by the action of
the Municipal Councils, which restricted their activities
in trade and handicrafts, and by that of the Diet, which
adopted several measures affecting Jewish commerce.
Thus, for instance, a law was passed in 1643 to the effect
that Jews might make a profit on imported goods
of only 3 per cent, foreigners of 5 per cent, and Polish
merchants of 7 per cent. It may be observed in passing
that from the point of view of the legislators a more stupid
law could not have been introduced, for it threw the buying
public into the arms of the Jewish trader. With regard to
customs also, there were separate tariffs for Catholics on
the one side, and for Jews and Lutherans on the other.
Whereas Catholic traders paid 8 per cent of the value
of imported goods and 10 per cent of the value of exported
articles, Jews and Lutherans had to pay 10 and 12 per cent
respectively.[1]

In the eighteenth century the overwhelming majority
of the Jewish population consisted of traders, artisans,
petty farmers and inn-keepers. We know from other
sources how extremely difficult was the position of this
mass of people. The Memoirs too present a gloomy picture
of the Jewish economic position in those days. The number
of individuals who were better off was negligible. Ber
may have belonged to this group, though he was by no
means a wealthy person. He earned enough to keep his
family decently, but in his later years he was in financial
straits. He had always to borrow money from nobles and
ecclesiastics, and so did many of his fellow-Jews. Times
had changed. The former debtors now became creditors
of the Jews. Ber's recollections provide most striking

---

[1] See *The History of the Jewish people* (R.), vol. XI, chapter 6: *Economic
conditions of the Jews in Poland and Lithuania*, by I. Schipper and M. Vishnitzer
Moscow, 1914, where further details will be found on this subject.

facts concerning the indebtedness of the Jewish traders
and farmers to the upper class of the Polish nation. There
is, on the contrary, scarcely any mention of Jews engaged
in money-lending. Our author refers to one of his teachers,
who used to lend money on pledges, pointing out at the
same time that this was a rather exceptional case. Curiously
enough, he was himself thinking of taking up this profession,
but was exhorted by his wife and relatives to abstain from
it; so he took to trade. After a few not unsuccessful
experiments in various branches he turned to dealing in
wine, which remained his chief occupation all his life.

With regard to the organisation of trade, we meet in
Ber's Memoirs with a form of company consisting of two,
three and sometimes even more partners. The system of
partnership was particularly necessary in the wine trade.
One member of the firm would travel to Hungary to
purchase wine, while the other had to stay at home to
look after the sale of the stocks. As to the conditions
under which the partners entered business, some interesting points are brought to light in the Memoirs. Another
form of partnership commonly met with in Ber's career
was his association with a sleeping partner, who handed
to Ber a certain amount for the purchase of wine, leaving
to him the whole conduct of the business. Noblemen and
ecclesiastics, chiefly the landlords of Bolechow, used to
undertake business as sleeping partners with Ber, or his
brother, or some other Jewish trader. We have before us
an example of a *Société en Commandite*. Ber, who was the
working partner, carried out the orders of those who
merely advanced the capital. There was, finally, a third
kind of commercial organisation — the agency. Count
Poniatowski, for instance, sent his clerk together with
Ber's father to buy wine in Hungary. In this case the
latter acted as agent, or rather expert (for Poniatowski
was informed that Ber's father was a connoisseur in the
wine trade), and received a reward for his services.

Our author sets out in a most graphic manner the experiences, the successes and the failures, which he had to

record in his long business career. His reputation must have been high, and his name well known. His business connections included Parisian and Warsaw firms, and among his customers we find members of the aristocracy, high officials, an officer of the Imperial Russian Court, and so forth. It was an extensive and ramified business which this Jewish·trader of Bolechow carried on, and he gives us a minute description of its various phases and episodes.

Goods were paid for either in money or in kind. Sometimes Ber paid partly in money and partly in goods. Bartering was on the whole very common in those years, as many examples quoted in the Memoirs show. Before going abroad the merchant had to procure foreign currency. Transactions were as a rule made against cash, and credit was but seldom given either by promissory notes or on the strength of personal confidence. Ber was careful to keep his account books in proper order, particularly when he conducted business in partnership. He liked order and system in a time of disorder and chaos. He was very exact, and even pedantic, in his affairs. His descriptions suggest a man of great accuracy, with a gift for the most minute observation. When he comes to report on a business transaction he is anxious not to omit the slightest detail of the sometimes lengthy negotiations. This makes his Memoirs all the more valuable.

Commerce — in particular the wine trade — is the chief topic of Ber's narrative, though some interesting side-lights are thrown upon other activities, and especially upon farming. His father was for some time a farmer of estates, he himself once held the lease of some of the revenues of the landlord of Bolechow, and certain of his contemporaries were professional leaseholders. The type of the enterprising Jewish farmer, which was so often met with in the sixteenth century, had almost died out two hundred years later, in the days of Ber. The time had gone by when public revenues were held on lease by Jewish· tenants, and it was only in the farming of private

property that Jews were engaged in the eighteenth century.
Of one of these farmers, who made a strong impression on
Ber, we are given an interesting picture. He was called
Saul Wal, like the famous social worker of the sixteenth
century who still lives in legend as the "Jewish King of One
Day". The Saul Wal described in the present Memoirs may
have been a descendant of the founder of that well-known
family. We learn from Ber that he was a man of ability
and high character, esteemed by Jews and non-Jews alike.
He had learnt agriculture in his early youth, and devoted
the larger portion of his life to the farming the estates of
nobles. But one day the landlord of the town of Stryi
and its surroundings told him that he did not care any
more for his tenantship. Ber describes the awful situation
of Wal and his large family. The poor man had not even
enough to repay the debts which he had incurred during a
period of years; and he would have been utterly ruined had
not Ber's father set him up in the wine business. We hear
also why it was that Wal lost his position. Count Poniatowski, who is otherwise known as a careful administrator,
decided to manage his estates himself, and to give up
letting them on lease, with the result that Wal lost his
livelihood.

The Jew, however, is versatile and quick to find a way
out of misfortune. Wal found another occupation, and so
did the other Jewish farmers and dealers in Poland. Often,
however, it was not so much that the Jew took to a
profession, as that the profession got hold of him. In
other words Jewish economic activities were determined
not by any special predilection, but by external conditions.
Ber's records illustrate this truth. He shows us that a
Jew was often constrained to take a lease from a noble
landlord, though it was clear as day that the lease must
be unprofitable. As has already been explained in another
connection, the Jews were indebted to the nobles, and
were often not in a position to meet their obligations.
In order to avoid vexations and the confiscation of his
goods, the debtor had to secure the protection of some

noble against his creditors. Ber, who was himself in this position, once found it worth while to lease the revenues of the town of Bolechow in order to be able to count on the assistance of his landlord in case his creditors should molest him. A more extreme case quoted by Ber shows that sometimes a Jew was even forcibly compelled to buy a lease from a noble, under the threat of expulsion from his native place. Such facts suggest reconsideration of the view sometimes advanced by historians, that the Jews took to farming as a profitable occupation. To judge from our author's and his contemporaries' experiences, this profession was not only often unable to provide a livelihood, but sometimes even involved considerable losses.[1]

The main callings of the Jews in those days were commerce, farming and crafts. We gather from our Memoirs abundant information concerning the commercial people, we obtain some insight into the position of the farmers, but we hear very little about Jewish craftsmen. The gap thus left open by the author in his economic picture is by no means a small one, for we know from other sources how numerous was the class of Jewish artisans in Ber's time, and we know also that they were organised in guilds, each craft in a separate guild. Some of these guilds, as, for instance, the Goldsmiths' guild at Lemberg, attained a high degree of efficiency and skill. This appears from Ber's incidental reference — and it is the only mention of Jewish craftsmanship in his Memoirs — to the opinion of an expert on the excellent work performed by that guild. A modern student of the history of Polish craftmanship also states that the Jewish guild of Goldsmiths at Lemberg had reached a high standard of perfection.[2] The Jewish artisans lived their separate

---

[1] The wretched position of the Jewish farmer is vividly described in the first chapters of the *Autobiography* of Solomon Maimon.

[2] W. Lozinski, in the *Records of the Commission for Investigation of the History of Art in Poland (P.)*, vol. V, pp. LXXVII—LXXVIII, quoted in my article *The Jewish Artisans and their Guild Organisation* (R.), in the *History of the Jewish People*, Moscow, 1914, vol. XI.

life, and mostly had their own synagogues. Ber was a merchant, and as such had no points of contact with the working men. This may explain his reticence on that branch of Jewish economic activities in the eighteenth century.

After this survey of economic and social conditions so far as they are illustrated by the Memoirs, a few general remarks on the organisation and inner life of the Jewish community in our author's day will complete this Introduction.

In early times in Poland the Jewish communities enjoyed the right of autonomous regulation of their own affairs. At the head of their communities stood elected bodies, called *Kahals*, whose functions covered a wide range of matters affecting religious life, legal questions, economic activities, fiscal duties, cultural needs and charitable institutions. The Government recognised the autonomous status of these bodies, and strengthened their authority, for fiscal reasons. The position was that taxes of the Crown were not paid by the Jews individually to the officials, but were collected by the *Kahals*, which were responsible for their due delivery to the Exchequer. In this way the *Kahals* obtained the position of public authorities, and in time became powerful. They were the representative organs of the communities in their multifarious relations with the State, the nobility, the burgesses, the clergy and even foreigners. All the threads of political and economic affairs with regard to the Jewish community converged in the offices of the *Kahals*. The administrative apparatus comprised various commissions, controllers and officers, such as clerks, beadles and tax-assessors. A special position was held by the Rabbis and Dayyans (Judges), who were also officers of the *Kahals*. They guided the community in religious and spiritual matters, and were the judges of the Jewish courts. The *Beth Din* was the competent Jewish Court in each community, and appeals could be made against its decisions to the Court of the Voyevoda or Palatine, who exercised control over the *Kahal* administration as a whole.

The position is illustrated by Ber's record of a case heard at the *Beth Din* at Lemberg, which shows that the judgment of this court was not valid without the assent of the Voyevoda.[1] The story as told by Ber is the more striking, as there was not even a formal appeal to the higher court, but an official of the Palatine was about to dismiss the Chief of the *Beth Din* on a charge of bribery brought by the relatives of a defendant who was dissatisfied with the judgment passed by the *Beth Din*. This instance illustrates the degeneration of the Jewish autonomous constitution in the eighteenth century, a period, as we have seen, of general political decline.

The whole power of the *Kahal* was concentrated in a small body of Wardens, or Elders, or Chiefs, usually four in number, who changed in rotation each month, and during that period were vested with full authority in administrative matters. They were accordingly called "Elders of the Month" (in Hebrew *Parnes Ha-Chodesh*, in Latin *Senior mensis*). The author of the Memoirs occupied this position in 1759, which was a very critical year in the annals of the Bolechow community. It was on the 9th July in that year that a band of ruffians broke into and plundered Jewish houses, killed several people and set many houses on fire. Incidentally we learn from Ber's dramatic narrative of this event that the band pushed into the Jewish houses early in the morning, after the guard, who had watched the whole night, had gone to rest. This was a Jewish guard, and we thus see that the *Kahal*, among its other duties, had to maintain a police force. The damage caused by the looting and the fire was very great, and the community was left in a desperate plight. The financial loss was so heavy that the community could not pay its taxes. In this calamity Ber proved himself

[1] The Voyevoda or Palatine, as the chief official of the province (voyevodship) was called, had control and jurisdiction over the Jewish communities. His court heard appeals which were made against the Jewish court or *Beth Din*.

an energetic and prudent communal leader. The various
stages of the lengthy negotiations with the authorities
concerning facilities for the payment of the taxes are
related in detail in the Memoirs, and there is no need to
dwell on them here. Where explanations are needed they
are given in the notes. Some remarks may, however, be
made in this connection with regard to Jewish fiscal
matters in general.

Reference is made in the Memoirs to the Jewish poll-
tax, to the excise of beer, mead and spirituous liquors
distilled from corn, to the "gabelle", a duty on ritual
slaughter, and some other minor levies. The poll-tax was
introduced in 1549, and was fixed in 1579 at 10,000 gulden
to be paid by the Jews in Poland and 3,000 by those in
Lithuania. Subsequently the demands of the Crown grew
ever greater, so that in the eighteenth century the Jews
in Poland had to pay 220,000 gulden and those in
Lithuania 60.000 gulden. Ber says that the amount of
the poll-tax reached 300,000 under an agreement made
between the Crown and the representatives of the Jews.
Though a poll-tax, it was not levied per head, but was
paid by the communities in equal shares, through the
medium of the Provincial Jewish Bodies, to the *Vaad*
or Council of Four Lands (the highest representative organ
of Polish Jewry), by which the taxes were finally delivered
to the State Treasurer's office. Complaint was made on
several occasions at the Polish Seyms or Diets that the
amounts paid by the Jewish autonomous bodies did not
correspond with the actual number of the Jewish population, and demands were put forward that this method
of taxation should be abolished and the poll-tax should
be levied directly on the individual Jew. The matter was
finally brought up at the Convocation Diet in 1764, which
preceded the election of King Stanislaus Poniatowski, and
a resolution was passed to the effect that henceforth the
Assemblies of the Jewish Central and Provincial Bodies
should be abolished and the poll-tax levied at a gulden
per head by the officials of the Crown. Moreover, a

general census of the Jewish population was carried out
in the years 1764 and 1765.[1] So far Ber's record of the
transition from the old to a new system of levying taxes
on the Jewish population is fairly in accordance with our
general knowledge of the facts. But he also mentions an
increase of the poll-tax to 3 gulden, though nothing is said
as to the date of this new decision, the duration of its
validity, or the provinces in which it was introduced.
The motives which led the Government to increase the
tax, as explained by Ber, are rather curious. According to
his information, the members of the dissolved Assemblies
presented a petition to the Crown, asking for the reimburse-
ment of the expenses which they had incurred during their
previous journeys to the sessions. The Government then
ordered the poll-tax to be increased to three gulden in
order to satisfy the claims of the petitioners from the
surplus sum. There is matter here for further investigation.
An increase of the tax to 3 gulden did indeed take place
in 1775, but this was at a time when Galicia had already
become an Austrian province, and Ber and his countrymen had ceased to be Polish subjects. Ber's reference to
an increase of the tax before 1773 needs to be corroborated
by some new piece of evidence.

The excise of beer, mead and spirituous liquors distilled
from corn was an indirect tax, introduced in 1629, which
fell on the Jewish inkeepers whose number so greatly
increased in the eighteenth century. This tax was later
on fixed at 10 per cent of the nett proceeds of the spirit
trade.

No exemption from Governmental taxes was made for
Jews residing on the estates of landlords and liable to their
jurisdiction and taxation. The landlords levied duties on
merchandise, on various articles of consumption, on ritual

[1] An exhaustive exposition of the fiscal system in Poland with regard
to taxation of Jews is to be found in the *History of the Jewish People*
(R.) already quoted, vol. XI, chapter 7, *Taxation*, by I. Schipper. See
also the article on the *Council of Four Lands* in the *Jewish Encyclopedia*,
vol. IV.

slaughter, etc. In this case too the Memoirs give us valuable information. The fiscal history of the Jewish communities in Poland is indeed an amazing record of a multiplicity of direct and indirect taxes, which would have been a heavy burden even to a population living under more favourable conditions than the contemporaries of Ber. The community of Bolechow, like so many others, was not in a position to meet all these demands, and petitioned the landlords for allowances; and abatements were made. Our author describes with a touch of humour the bargaining for reductions of taxes. His sketches of the fiscal troubles of his community vividly illustrate the feudalistic conditions of that time.

The economic position of the Jews became in time appalling. The number of paupers outgrew the people capable of paying taxes. The Crown, however, levied the poll-tax on all Jews without regard to their earning capacity. The community of Bolechow decided at one time, on the advice of our author, to conceal from the authorities the real numbers of the Jewish population, in order to save the poor people from payment; and two prominent members of the community were compelled to swear in the Court that the figures given by the communal authorities were accurate.

The Central and Provincial Jewish Bodies regularly met in Assemblies with the object of discussing matters of general interest to the whole Jewish community in Poland and Lithuania, and issued decisions and regulations which were binding on the communities. The autonomous constitution of the Polish and Lithuanian Jews may be compared with a pyramid. At the base stood the communities, higher up the provincial bodies, and on the top the central organisations, the *Vaads*, or Councils, one for Poland and one for Lithuania. The Rabbinical members of the Assemblies formed the Supreme Courts, which heard lawsuits between communities and individuals and between one community and another. The author of the Memoirs dwells rather sympathetically on the activities of these various organs of Jewish autonomy in Poland, and gives a vivid picture of the proceedings of the Assemblies. His statement that these institutions were 800 years old is, however, incorrect, as we know that the first Assemblies of representatives of Jewish communities in Poland did not meet before the sixteenth century. Another statement deserves more attention. Ber tells us that he had seen in his youth printed copies of the decisions of the Assemblies. If Ber is not mistaken, these books were lost afterwards, for we do not possess a single copy to-day. What we have are manuscript minutes of the Lithuanian Jewish Assembly or *Vaad*, which have only been published recently, while the minutes of the Polish Assembly, except for a few sheets, have not even been preserved in manuscript. Several decisions arrived at in the Polish Vaad happen to be included in communal records and in various rabbinical works.

In 1764, as we have already seen, the Jewish provincial and central bodies were dissolved by the Government. Besides the purely fiscal grounds for this decision, there was, according to Ber, another reason. The suspension of the Polish Diets had become, as we have seen, a chronic disease. Very seldom could a session be finished, for in most cases a deputy would rise and exclaim "I disapprove". This deputy was always the mouthpiece of the aristocratic factions, who in turn were tools in the hands of foreign ambassadors. It was in the interests of Poland's neighbours, especially Russia, that the constitutional machinery of the country should not work. That the Jews had instigated these suspensions of the Diets was insinuated in some political pamphlets of the eighteenth century, and was alleged in certain sections of the nobility. Ber directs our attention to this question, for he heard such opinions emanating from noble circles. Their arguments were as follows: The Jews were afraid of any legislative measures of the Diets which might be adopted with the object of restricting their economic activities; therefore, they bribed individual deputies in order to "explode" the sessions of the Diet. This danger, the nobles thought, could be averted if the Jewish Assemblies, which sent their representatives to Warsaw during the sessions of the Diets, were abolished. These arguments of the Polish nobility, as transmitted by our author, are too naive and too obviously remote from any contact with reality to be worth criticism. The bishop of Kiev, Samuel Ozga, in a letter addressed to the King in 1740, attributed the decline of the Diet to foreign machinations, and it is interesting to note that in mentioning the Jews as a factor which also prevented the proceedings of that session of the Diet in 1740 from being concluded he quotes vaguely as authority "public rumour".[1] This proves once more that the accusation had no real foundations, and that the source of these rumours was enmity towards the Jews. But in any case, if we follow our memoir-writer we gather that these charges, in conjunction with the demand for a more efficient system of taxation of the Jews, led to the dissolution of the Jewish Assemblies.[2]

Our author was very grieved at the abolition of the Assemblies, as they were "a small solace to the children of Israel, and a little honour too, and witnesses that God in his great pity had not deserted us". He could not help seeing in the first partition of Poland (1772) God's punishment for the disgrace suffered by the Jews when they were bereft of their autonomous status. His usually sober intellect was in this instance mastered by his feelings, and he wrote bitterly. We know, however, from other Jewish sources that the partition of Poland occasioned great dismay.[3]

Ber's record is a vivid picture of the manners and customs of his time. We are somewhat surprised to learn

---

[1] See L. Glatman, *Historical Sketches (P.)*, Cracow, 1906, p. 111.

[2] Some meetings, however, took place afterwards, for the purpose of the liquidation of old affairs. Ber refers to a conference of representatives of the district of Lemberg, and gives a list of the delegates, omitting, however, the date.

[3] S. Bennett, *The Constancy of Israel*, London, 1809, p. 218.

from it that the Polish Jews were accustomed to making
distant journeys on horseback, sometimes accompanied
by a Christian groom. Even rabbis were used to ride.
We further learn that Jews handled firearms. Their intercourse with their Christian environment is illustrated by
accounts of Gentiles accepting invitations from Jews and
visiting wineshops in Jewish company. That Jewish wo-
men were fond of fashionable and expensive frocks is a
feature mentioned by Ber in a dry, matter-of-fact way.
Many little traits illustrative of Jewish usages and valuable
for Jewish folklore are to be found here and there.

Memoirs deal with men and things. Ber belongs to the
class of memoirists who deal more with things, events and
institutions than with persons. His remarks on prominent
contemporaries, on Rabbis, on communal leaders, on his
family, are rather short, but they are expressive and
comprehensive. Mention is made of a few scores of names,
both of the Jewish and non-Jewish contemporaries of the
author. Most of these names are but little known, and
are therefore of insignificant interest even to students of
history, except a few specialists. The index at the end
of this book includes all the names, and will facilitate the
use of the Memoirs for research work. Here we need
mention only a couple of Rabbis, scholars and communal
leaders, who either appear for the first time on the public
platform thanks to Ber's record, or are otherwise already
known by their activities in Jewish cultural and social life.

Rabbi Ḥayyim Cohen Rapaport, Chief Rabbi of Lemberg, was a great Rabbinical authority in the eighteenth
century. We marvel together with his biographers at his
vast and deep erudition in Jewish Law, we know that his
fame spread throughout Poland and abroad, and we re-
collect with gratitude the courage which he displayed in
the defence of the Jewish faith against the accusations
brought by the sect of the Frankists. This remarkable
man became a friend of Ber, who in 1752 was able, thanks
his knowledge of Polish, to render him a very valuable
service by saving him from being expelled from Lemberg.

The description of this episode occupies a considerable
portion of the Memoirs. Subsequently our author remained
in close relations with Rabbi Ḥayyim Rapaport, and his
knowledge of Polish was again of assistance to the Rabbi,
this time in a joint effort in the cause of Judaism.

When Ber and his brother Aryeh Loeb arrived in
Lemberg, on the 23rd August 1759, to look after their
wine business, they learned that the Jewish community
was in great distress. The disputation with the Frankists,
which had begun on the 17th July under the auspices
of Bishop Mikulski, and had been attended by 40 Rabbis
and communal leaders, had been adjourned at the request
of the Frankists. Ber examined the position, and, together
with his brother, had a long conversation with the members
of the cathedral chapter, in the course of which they succeeded in opening the eyes of the priests to the real aims
of the sectarians, whose eagerness to be converted to
Christianity was due solely to the material advantages
which they expected to obtain from their noble godfathers.
The priests then decided to hasten on the disputation,
which was fixed for the 27th August. It was one of the
usual scholastic tournaments of Mediaeval times, rich in
subtleties and quibbling. In these days of critical research
it appears absurd that the interpretation of this or that
sentence or expression in a Biblical or Talmudical text
could provoke an emotional outburst; but we must recall
the atmosphere of theological disputes in those days of
religious intollerance, an atmosphere in which the defeated
party felt so intensely the results of the oral duel. The
representatives of the Jews were aware of the grave con-
sequences which would have followed for the Jewish community had they failed to be victors. Rabbi Rapaport
and Ber, his interpreter, defeated the embittered sectarians,
and the fast-day ended for the Jews with a feeling of relief.
Ber composed, at the Rabbi's request, a written refutation
of the theses of the Frankists. This statement was in part
published in Polish in 1760, and has recently been printed
in the Hebrew original, as part of one of Ber's works

which deals with the Jewish sectarian movements.[1] In the Memoirs too Ber dwells to some extent "on the great and famous disputation which took place at Lemberg between all Israel on the one side, and the sect of the believers in Shabbetai Zebi, be his name extirpated, on the other side".[2]

The family of Hurwitz has produced many Rabbis, some of whom have attained to fame. We find representatives of this family occupying the Rabbinical chair at Bolechow. Mention has already been made of Yukel Hurwitz[3], whose farewell address in the open air left such an indelible impression on the author of the Memoirs. This speech is reproduced from memory by Ber, and may serve as a specimen of Rabbinical preaching in the first decades of the eighteenth century. Rabbi Yukel Hurwitz appears here as a witty preacher and a man with an understanding of practical life. His son Mordecai succeeded him as Rabbi at Bolechow, but died after a year. So great was the attachment of the community to this Rabbi that the seat was left vacant for a whole year, and his full salary was paid to his widow. Another Hurwitz was then invited to occupy the Rabbinical chair at Bolechow, a certain Moses, son of Aaron. This Moses remained for ten years at Bolechow. "He enjoyed" says Ber "great consideration, for he carried out his duties with wisdom, in face of the opposition of some leading people in the community". It is a pity that Ber was not more explicit, for the question of the mutual relationship of the Rabbis and the *Kahals* is an intricate subject. The internal peace of the community was very often clouded by dissensions and quarrels between its spiritual and lay heads, and sometimes, as for example at Cracow and Vilna, these dissensions assumed a very unpleasant aspect.

[1] See Dr. A. Brawer, in *Hashiloah*, 1917, vol. 38, pp. 349—354. On pp. 16—21 and pp. 231—238 Ber's report of the disputation is given fully.

[2] Jacob Frank was a follower of the pseudo-Messiah Shabbetai Zebi.

[3] Ch. D. Friedberg, *The History of the Family Hurwitz* (H). Frankfurt (on the Main) 1911.

Ber appears to have had no great opinion of the Jewish communal leaders and representatives whom he mentions in his Memoirs. He criticises their activities, and is particularly insistent in pointing out the inefficiency of the Jewish Elders of Bolechow in dealing with complicated questions and in pleading the cause of their community before the Polish authorities and those Jewish bodies which, as we have seen, stood above the communities. Ber speaks sarcastically of a member of the communal hierarchy who failed to discharge an important mission to the State Treasurer because he did not know how to reply to the arguments of the Treasurer, and showed himself "illiterate as a calf". On other occasions also Ber pours scorn on the communal leaders. In marked contrast is his appreciation of the merits of his elder brother, Aryeh Loeb, as a social worker. No praise is too great for the cleverness, eloquence, courtesy and goodness of this marvellous man, who had taken a prominent part in the Jewish affairs of the district of Lemberg, and had been unanimously elected President or Marshal of the Provincial Jewish Assembly. From what we hear elsewhere in the Memoirs, he must have had a fine reputation and have enjoyed the confidence of the people. He was a man whose counsel was sought in critical hours, and who was asked to go when necessary to Warsaw to plead before the authorities there. The sources of Jewish communal history in those years are unfortunately very poor, so that we are unable to confirm Ber's statements by other evidence; and for the same reason we are not in a position to say anything more about one or two other leading members of that Provincial Assembly, whom Ber mentions with respect.

We do not know exactly when the Memoirs were written, but it was clearly not before 1790, for our author speaks of the Emperor Joseph II as deceased. Moreover, as he appends to the name of nearly every man and woman mentioned in the Memoirs the words "Be his (or her) memory blessed", he must have outlived almost all his relatives, friends and acquaintances; and this suggests that he wrote his Memoirs in his old age. In 1800 he composed a treatise on the Jewish religion and sects called *Dibre Binah*,[1] and in the present Memoirs he tells us that he intends writing a book against the slanderers of the Jewish faith, which, we assume, is identical with the *Dibre Binah*. We may, therefore, take it that the Memoirs were written between 1790 and 1800, when Ber was about eighty years old. Only the first fifty years of his busy and eventful life are described, and even in this period there are certain gaps, particularly as regards the years 1743—1773. However, we obtain sufficient insight into that period of Ber's life which ended in the flower of his manhood.

Nothing is said in the Memoirs as to the views and impressions of the author in his later years, that is to say, in the last three decades of the eighteenth century, which witnessed so many vital changes in the social and cultural life of the Jews in Galicia. This deplorable gap is partly filled by a few glimpses which we obtain from Ber's *Dibre Binah*. We learn from this work that our author never belonged to those bitter antagonists of *Hasidism*,[2] who in their narrow-minded orthodoxy persecuted the adherents of the mystical mass movement, and did not shrink from provoking strife and trouble in the Jewish communities. On the contrary, Ber in his old age was grieved at these outrages of intolerance, and was anxious to restore peace in the excited communities. So far from hating the preachers of the new doctrine, the *Hasidic* Rabbis, he treated them hospitably and supported them materially; but he did not care much for their mystical revelations or their teaching. He regarded them as successors of the *Baale Shem*,[3]

---

[1] See Dr. Brawer, in *Hashiloah*, vol. 33 p. 149.

[2] See Dr. Brawer, *loc. cit.*, p. 152—153. — *Hasidism* is a religious mystical movement which began in Poland among the Jews in the eighteenth century, and found great numbers of believers owing to the fact that it appealed to sentiment and was hostile to religious dogmatism. See S. Dubnow, in the *Jewish Encyclopedia*, vol. VI.

[3] "People who represented a mixture of quack doctor, physician and cabbalist" (*Jewish Encyclopedia*, vol. II, p. 382—383).

and quarrelled with them on account of their innovations
in the service, but this was far from the intransigent
attitude of the extreme adversaries of Ḥasidism. The same
leaning to moderation may be observed in the appreciation
shown in the *Dibre Binah* of the Western tendencies represented in the *Haskalah*. Ber was alarmed at the strange
behaviour of the pioneers of this movement, at their cynical
infringement of religious commandments, and feared that
these practices would lead to desertion from the faith. With all
his love of general knowledge and broad-minded education,
he remained at the same time deeply attached to Judaism.
In this respect he was a pioneer of enlightenment, a living
example to his age of a man conversant both with Jewish
and with non-Jewish learning. It is this which makes his
personality so interesting in the study of Jewish cultural
life in the eighteenth century.

There has always been a genuine respect for and attachment to general knowledge among Polish Jewry. This
spirit was strong already in the sixteenth century, when
the love of philosophic research gave rise to the famous
clash of opinions which occured in the community of
Posen.[1] It was perhaps overshadowed by cabbalistic pursuits in the following century, though the zeal for criticism
did not subside even then; and we see a revival of the
attachment to general culture in the eighteenth century.
Our author is, as we pointed out above, one example
among many others. The pioneers of intellectual progress
in the period under consideration included such men as
Israel Zamosc (1700—1772), teacher of Mendelssohn and
author of books on mathematics, physics, astronomy and
philosophy, Doctor Abraham Usiel, a physician who completed his studies in Germany,[2] and Mendel Satanower,
a mathematician and a popular Hebrew writer on natural

[1] S. P. Rabinovitch, *The Traces of Free Thought in Polish Rabbinism*
(R.) in the quarterly *Jewish Antiquity* (R.), Petrograd, 1911, pp. 1—19.

[2] N. M. Gelber, *Aus dem Pinax des alten Judenfriedhofes in Brody*, in
Jahrbuch der Jüdisch-Literarischen Gesellschaft, Frankfurt, 1920, p. 132.
Brawer, in *Hashiloaḥ*, vol. 33, 149; vol. 38, 237.

science, who was anxious to enlighten the masses, and to that end planned a translation of the Bible into Yiddish.[1] As the eighteenth century drew to its close, new adepts joined this movement. In 1797 there appeared an encyclopaedic work in Hebrew, *Sefer Ha-Berith*, by Elijah, son of Pinchas Vilna, a native of Lemberg. This book embraced various scientific and philosophical subjects, including the system of Kant.[2] The Rabbis Solomon, son of Moses, and Salman Margulies, who advocated the adoption of a systematic method in Jewish learning, and were by no means averse from general studies,[3] are also among the outstanding personalities of that progressive epoch. These are only a few names in the comparatively small area of Eastern Galicia. And what of those whose names have not been preserved, whose writings have been lost, or have never been printed? What of that Joseph Kopel whose books were on the shelves of Ber, his devoted friend and admirer? What of the other literary men at Tysmienica whose intercourse our author so much enjoyed in his youth? There seems to have existed an intense cultural life in those Galician communities, the full extent of which we shall not comprehend until more light has been thrown on that period by students of history.

Ber died on 10th March, 1805, at Bolechow, and was buried there.[4] Little is known of his offspring. His eldest son, Joshua, who appears in the Memoirs as a very clever boy and in poor health, died in his father's life. Another son, Joseph, who had been married to a daughter of Joseph Kopel, was alive when the Memoirs were written. No other mention is made of Ber's children.[5]

---

[1] N. M. Gelber, *Mendel Satanower, der Verbreiter der Haskalah in Polen und Galizien*, in *Mitteilungen für Jüdische Volkskunde, 1914*.

[2] M. Weissberg, *Die Neuhebräische Aufklärungsliteratur in Galizien*, p. 10.

[3] idem, *loc. cit.*, p. 11.

[4] His grave is situated in the old part of the cemetery among the tombs of the then prominent Jews of Bolechow. The inscription on the tombstone is plain and short. Ber Birkenthal is described in it as "the learned, the renowned leader, the open-handed, the aged".

[5] Dr. Brawer, *op. cit.* in *Hashiloaḥ* vol. 33, p. 153, says that a daughter of Ber was married to Dr. Yakobka Rapaport "who was a famous physician

Diaries and memoirs written by ordinary people, that is to say by persons who did not belong to the ruling classes and have nothing to do with politics and warfare, will ever possess a peculiar charm and value. History appears in such writings as though observed from bypaths. Memoirists like Ber relate events as they occurred from day to day, without the generalisations dictated by official reasons or party bias. Polish and Jewish historiography are rather poor in sources of this kind. A diary of a Cracow merchant of the seventeenth century, John Markiewicz, fragmentarily written in his ledger of payments and expenses,[1] and Ber's autobiographical sketches, are, so far as we know, the only records of this type.

Ber's reminiscences will in my opinion rank in the annals of Jewish historiography as a lucid and trustworthy account of an insufficiently explored chapter of our past. They will be added to the *Memoirs of Glueckel of Hameln*, the *Autobiography of Solomon Maimon* and the *Megillat Sefer* of Jacob Emden as an authentic specimen of that type of literature.[2] If we consider the rich store of facts and events, the insight into political and social conditions, and finally, the detailed descriptions of public

at Lemberg". According to Wurzbach, *Biographisches Lexikon des Kaisertums Österreich*, a Dr. Jacob Rapaport was born in 1775 in Uman (in the Ukraine) and died in 1855 at Lemberg. He became Doctor in 1804, a year before Ber's death. My friend, Dr. M. Balaban, writes to me that according to his notes on the epitaphs of the Lemberg Cemetery Rapaport's wife was called Juliana and died in her 65th year, in 1848.

[1] See L. Kubala, *A Polish burgess of the 17th century*, in vol. II of *Historical Sketches* (P), pp. 285 *sq.*

[2] In recent years there have been published more memoirs and autobiographical records, as, for instance, those of the Warden of the Berlin community A. H. Heymann (*Lebenserinnerungen*, edited by Heinrich Loewe, 1909), of the Viennese business man S. Meyer (*Memoiren eines jüdischen Kaufmanns*, 1906), of Paulina Wengeroff (*Memoiren einer Großmutter*, 1908), who depicted the conditions of Russian Jewry in the nineteenth century, of a certain Moses Wasserzug (*Memoiren eines polnischen Juden*, edited by Heinrich Loewe, 1911) and of other writers and social workers, whose memoirs, however, touch upon the life of the Jews in the last decades of the nineteenth century.

and private life which Ber's Memoirs present, this document may be regarded as of more intrinsic value for historical research than the other three works mentioned. Solomon Maimon wrote in German, Glueckel of Hameln in Judaeo-German or Yiddish, Jacob Emden and Ber in Hebrew. Ber wrote in a simple, vigorous and unaffected style, unlike the writers of his time, whose language was flowery and artificial. He is far from being jejune; on the contrary, he keeps the reader interested by the easy flow of his narrative. The Memoirs of Ber are not only an instructive document, but also an entertaining piece of literature.

THE MEMOIRS OF BER OF BOLECHOW.

. . . . At[1] the same time he[2] was carrying on a trade
in Hungarian wine. He ordered a suitable cellar to be
excavated and built for preserving wines. Every year
he sold these wines at a considerable price to the nobles,
who lived on their estates near Bolechow; and he made
a fortune. And there I was born, as stated before on p. . .[3]
As the soil of the estates, which were situated in the
mountains, was not capable of producing fruit, my father
was induced to commence another business with the
peasants, the serfs of his tenantry. He made an agreement
with the leaseholder of the salt-springs at Bolechow to
furnish him with timber from the forest. A cartload of
timber delivered at the salt-springs was exchanged for
a barrel of salt of good quality, This was carried on
during the whole of the winter, and many barrels of salt
were collected in this way. When summer came, and the
fruit of the fields began to ripen, the serfs from the villages
took their carts and loaded every cart with ten barrels
of salt, and went into the district of Podolia, where they
exchanged the salt for corn, that is to say, one barrel of
salt for one barrel of corn, and sometimes for one-and-
a-half or even two barrels of corn. From this corn liquors
were distilled, which were bought and carried into Hungary
in great quantities, and the profit realised on this transaction amounted to a nice sum of money, in addition to
that from the Hungarian wine trade. In this way my
father became affluent and was highly respected; this went

[1] The Manuscript as we have it begins with the word "villages", which
is evidently the end of a sentence.

[2] Refers to the author's father.

[3] Not preserved.

on for six years. There I was born, and my brother Seeb Wolf, be his memory for a blessing,[1] and Loeb, my sister's son, as stated on p. . .[2]

At that time my father bought a house in Bolechow from the *Aluf*[3] R. David, son of R. Baruch. It was an old building, and my father enlarged it by more than a half by a new and beautiful extension; the construction was finished in 487 (1727).[4] The date can be seen to this day on the vane on the top of the roof at the back of the house; in the centre of the vane, which was made of tin, there are the letters תפ"ז (that is, 487). In the grounds of the house situated next to ours on the east side was a brewery, with a large cauldron for preparing mead and beer, which belonged at that time to the landlord of Bolechow. My father bought this brewery from the wife of the castellan of Liw,[5] *Pani*[6] Cieszkowska, who then owned the estate of Bolechow. This brewery and the two large cauldrons which have been hitherto in my possession brought in good revenues. May the Lord favour us with such for long years.

When the house was completed the wedding took place of my distinguished and learned brother, R. Axelrod Bendet, with his bride Braine, the daughter of the famous Dayyan of the community of Lemberg, R. Nathan Nate, who was well-known as R. Nate, son of R. Meshulam, of the inner town of Lemberg.[7]

---

[1] The words "Be his (or her) memory for a blessing" appear after the names of nearly every person mentioned in the Memoirs. The author had outlived nearly all his relatives and friends. (See also note 4 on p. 67.)

[2] Not preserved.

[3] A person who enjoyed high rank in the Jewish communal hierarchy.

[4] See note 2 on p. V of the Preface.

[5] The widow of the castellan of Liw, Victor Felix Cieszkowski landlord of Bolechow. The office of castellan was a purely honorary position; the holders of castellanships were senators.

[6] The designation of the wives of Polish nobles.

[7] There were two Jewish communities in Lemberg — the community in the inner town and that on the outskirts. — See S. Buber, *Anshé Shem* 1895, where, however, the name of R. Nate's father is given as Reuben.

The position of the landlords of Bolechow — they were of the family of Giedzinski[1] — became precarious, and so they were forced to sell their estates in order to repay the debts they had incurred. A new Count, named Poniatowski, the father of King Augustus Poniatowski, then came forward, and laid out all the money which was required for the purchase of this estate, a sum of 600,000 Polish gulden.[2]

Count Poniatowski was granted by the King the estate of Stryi[3] and promoted to be the Starosta[4] of that town. Then the landlords of Bolechow, who (as has been said) were in great financial straits, sold the town of Bolechow and the surrounding land to Count Poniatowski with a view to repaying their debt, which amounted to a sum of 600,000 gulden.

Then it was that the four chiefs of the Polish army died, that is, the Grand Hetman[5] and the Field Hetman of Poland, and the Grand Hetman and the Field Hetman of Lithuania. And they all passed away.[6] The King of Poland and Elector of Saxony, Augustus I,[7] showed a disposition to elevate Count Poniatowski and to bestow wealth and honour on him. After having filled for some years the office of State Treasurer of Lithuania,[8] Poniatowski was promoted to the position of Commander in Chief of the Polish forces[9] in place of the four

[1] See Adam Boniecki and Artur Rejski, *Polish Heraldry* (P.), 1912, vol. VI, p. 39.

[2] Or florin, in Polish — *złot.* W. Coxe, *Travels into Poland, Denmark etc.* (1784—1790), estimates the value of the Polish gulden at nearly 6 d. See also Introduction, p. 26.

[3] Town in Galicia.

[4] The chief executive officer of the local administration.

[5] B. Connor, *A Comprehensive Account of the Kingdom of Poland*, 1744, says: Grand General.

[6] Not quite correct. In 1728 three of the Hetmans died, viz., Stanislaus Chomentowski, Grand Hetman of Poland, Stanislaus Rzewuski, Field Hetman of Poland, and Stanislaus Denhof, Field Hetman of Lithuania.

[7] Correctly Augustus II.

[8] Appointed in 1724.

[9] In Polish: *Generalny Regimentarz.*

Hetmans who had died. Although I know the history and the particulars of the activities of various Polish nobles and even of the Polish kings, as I have had opportunities of looking into their historical books, I forbear to burden the reader with too many details.

———————

...... to sell them for a sum less than 25 ducats; and we did not purchase any of the old wines. I was very disappointed at not being able to obtain any of the old wines. I discussed the matter with my partner on our way from Miskolcz,[1] as I had no other opportunity of doing so, because I had to return to Lemberg to see if the wines which were in the care of R. Isaac, my partner's brother, and under the control of my brother, the learned R. Bendet Axelrod, had been sold. R. Jacob[2] had to remain with the cartloads to look after the (newly acquired) wines. When we took leave of each other after we had left Miskolcz early on Sunday morning, I said to him: "I know that there are available a great number of casks of good old wine at Stryi with the *Kazin*[3] R. Hirsch, son of R. Mordechai, these wines being of 509 (1749). I possess samples of these good old wines at Lemberg; they came into my hands through my brother, R. Aryeh Loeb, who was empowered by R. Hirsch to sell those wines at Lemberg, because there were no buyers at Stryi. Those samples are still preserved in our wine-cellar at Lemberg. Therefore, on my way through Stryi, I should like to visit the owner of the wines, look into the vaults, sample the goods and arrange a fair price. Perhaps I might be able to buy some of the casks of that wine, so that we might have a greater variety of goods, as every vintner ought to have." And I did as I said, when I had reached Stryi. I tasted the wines and left a letter for my partner, asking him to take

[1] Town in Hungary.
[2] The author's partner.
[3] A person of wealth, position and influence in the community.

one of the four casks of the good old wines, which I found
with the wine merchant, R. Hirsch, with whom I had
discussed the price but had come to no agreement. I sealed
with my own seal the chosen cask of wine, requesting
that it be kept until the arrival of R. Jacob, so that he
might finally arrange the price and take the wine with him.
R. Jacob arrived and bought the wine I had chosen for
the sum of 26 ducats. He brought it with the other wines
and placed them all in our wine-vaults in a house built
of bricks, which belonged to the Carmelite Monastery.

This happened just before the fairs, and we heard that
the date of the wedding of the daughter of Count Branicki,
the Castellan of Wizna, was approaching. She was betrothed
to the son of Prince Sapieha, the Voyevoda of Smolensk.[1]
Count Branicki, the Castellan, was staying in the house of
Doctor Goranie, opposite the "Gate of Halicz" and near
the brick house, which was our inn. Some of the Castellan's
domestics were gentle people from our neighbourhood, and
knew us very well. They used their influence so that all
the wines required for the wedding were bought from us
— many casks of ordinary wine. But when my partner
arrived from Stryi with the old wine, we filled three *antals*[2]
(or barrels), which Prince Sapieha also bought from us
for 51 ducats. As soon as this sale was accomplished,

---

[1] Niesiecki, *Herbarz Polski*, 1871, I, 285 and II, 283, refers to the marriage
of Elisabeth, daughter of Peter Branicki, castellan of Braclaw, with John,
the son of Paul Peter Sapieha, Voyevoda of Smolensk. Ber is thus accurate
except in referring to Branicki as Castellan of Wizna, which was one of
the lesser castellanships in Poland. In the full list of the castellans given
by Niesiecki in his first volume, Peter Branicki appears among those of
Braclaw, but there is no reference to a Branicki among the Castellans of Wizna.

[2] According to Linde, *Dictionary of the Polish Language* (P.), the fourth
part of a cask of 18 pots. Other evidence (quoted by A. Fournier, *Handel
und Verkehr in Ungarn und Polen um die Mitte des XVIII. Jahrhunderts* in
Archiv für Österreichische Geschichtskunde, vol. 69) shows that the *Antheyl*,
as this measure was called in Central Europe, included 25 or 27 pots, and
that two antals equalled one cask. Ber used to make sometimes two and
sometimes three antals from one cask. According to Connor, *op. cit.*, the
Polish pot was about three quarts.

R. Jacob went over to Stryi, bought the three other casks of good wine from R. Zebi Hirsch for 90 ducats, and brought them to Lemberg. We transferred the three casks into nine barrels, and sold each barrel for 18 ducats, save two barrels, which remained in our wine-cellar another year.

We then agreed to travel to Hungary to purchase some more of its excellent old vintage. But as we still had a great quantity of wine in our vaults, it was inopportune to shut up the vaults; on the contrary, it was necessary for me to stay behind in order to attend to our usual customers, the nobles. So I remained at Lemberg. My partner, R. Jacob, took a sum of nearly 1000 ducats from our capital, and went alone to make purchases on our joint account. He bought 80 casks, which he brought to Skole.[1] It happened that at that time there was in that town an Armenian winetrader from Kamieniec, who tasted all the wines and chose eight casks of good old wine called *máslás*.[2] My partner sold them to the Armenian at a good profit, but he deceived me, telling me neither of the purchase nor of the selling of these casks of wine. On the contrary, he only showed me the account of the purchase of 72 casks of very inferior vintage, which he placed in our cellars at Lemberg. There was no sale for these wines, until one noble bought thirteen casks; and we had to sell him also two barrels of the old wine which we had from R. Hirsch of Stryi. This noble paid us with articles of gold and silver set with precious stones and diamonds rare and valuable. The rest of the wine remained a long time in our cellars without being sold.

It can easily be seen that the deception practised by my partner deprived me of the good income which I had been making. First, he bought eight casks of excellent Hungarian wine and sold them to the Armenian trader

---

[1] Township south of Stryi in Galicia.

[2] A variety of wine to be met with in the neighbourhood of Tokay. See *Encyclopaedia Britannica*, vol. XXVIII, p. 728.

without telling me about it. I did not know the quality
of the wine or how much he paid for it, but he made a
good profit on these eight casks of wine, certainly over
100 ducats. Then he took from our common capital
1000 gulden for his own use, and refused to account for
it. He went so far as to take my share, not being satisfied
with withholding from my knowledge the transaction with
the Armenian. His wife Beila also came to Lemberg
to help her husband to rob me of my livelihood.
They forgot the favours I had done them during the five
years we had been in partnership. Before our partnership
they were people of little means, but now their income
was increasing, thanks to the Almighty, through my
perseverance in and my knowledge of business affairs,
and besides this I was the means of getting both his
children successfully married. The young Blima was
married at my suggestion to the son of the Rabbi and
preacher of Lemberg, the Gaon R. Moses, who had been
previously President of the *Beth Din* of Tomaszow.[1] His son,
R. Judah (Blima's husband), was Rabbi at Zurawno and
later at Skole.[2] Jacob was very pleased with this marriage,
and though usually a great miser, he gave me 10 ducats
for my favourable speech on his behalf. For his only son
Sisie I arranged a very good match with the daughter
of R. Elieser Menkis. There was no other marriage broker
connected with this affair, and I myself worked to bring
about the alliance between these families. To show their
appreciation of my efforts both families made me a present
of a pair of gold earrings set with precious stones, the
value of which was 8 ducats. In spite of all this, R. Jacob
and his wife forgot the kindness I showed them, and now
they were bent on robbing me. I said to myself that this

---

[1] See S. Buber, *Anshé Shem*, 1895, (H), p. 167—168. Gaon was the
title of the Heads of the Talmudical Academies in Sura and Pumbadita, in
Babylon. In the eighteenth century this title was revived and applied to
nearly every Rabbi. See *Jewish Encyclopedia*, vol. VI. Gaon.

[2] Concerning the literary activities of this R. Judah see Buber, *op. cit.*,
p. 167.

was really one of the favours sent by God, blessed be He, Whose will it is that "the rod of the wicked shall not rest upon the lot of the righteous".[1] So I decided to separate. One night a sentence from the Bible came into my head. It was from Psalm 58, verse 5: "Their poison is like the poison of a serpent: they are like the deaf adder that stoppeth her ear; which will not hearken to the voice of charmers". That was R. Jacob; he was deaf, and would not listen to the voice of the teachers who advised him to keep on the right path. Further it is written in verse 9: "As a snail which melteth, let every one of them pass away: like the untimely birth of a woman, that they may not see the sun." That was his wife, the accursed woman Beila, who stirred up strife and contention between us. This made me very angry, and brought me to the decision to dissolve the partnership at the right time. After this I used to recite Psalm 58 with great devotion every day, during the morning and evening prayers.

But now we will return to the story of the affairs of my elder brother, the *Kazin* R. Aryeh Loeb, after he had separated from me and our partnership had been dissolved; this partnership having lasted for three years to our happiness and success. My brother travelled alone to Hungary for the purpose of purchasing wines, taking with him a considerable sum of money. He bought about 50 casks of wine, good to the taste, but somewhat clouded in colour, owing to a great amount of sediment, and it was impossible to sell it in that condition. But God sent the healing before the plague. The man who chopped our wood and brought our water — previously employed in a brick house of a wine trader in Lemberg — told us what his master used to do with wine in this condition. He filtered the wine through flax sacks spread over empty casks, and so the wine became clear and clean. I advised my brother to follow this example, which he did, and he was thus able to sell his wine. Then he made preparations to travel

[1] Ps. 125 ³.

again to Hungary for the purchase of more wines, and
I arranged that my partner, R. Jacob, should go with
him, in order that I might be informed by my brother
about the doings of R. Jacob in Hungary. The *Kazin*
R. Zebi Hirsch, son of R. Mordechai, of Stryi, also went
with them to buy wine. They came to Miskolcz, and
each one purchased the wines which he required.

At the same time there also arrived there wine traders
from the town of Dukla, who bought considerable quantities of wine; the *Kazin* R. Ḥayyim of Dukla [1] in particular made a large purchase. He paid the Hungarian merchants in ducats, all of which proved, however, to be
bad, and the edges were of copper — really brass coins.
The Hungarians were very angry at this, and informed
the Governor and the judges of the town, showing them
the coins trimmed and alloyed with inferior metal; under
the gold cover there was nothing but copper. R. Ḥayyim
and R. Hirsch were at once summoned to the Court to
answer to the charge. In the meantime the waggons loaded
with my brother's wines left the town on their way home;
only my brother and my partner remained at Miskolcz,
making their final preparations before following the
waggons. Then R. Hirsch came to my brother, asking him
to be so kind as to go to the Court and vouch for his
innocence, and to support him with evidence. My brother,
who had been from childhood of a very obliging nature,
always ready to do a kindness to anybody, could not
refuse this request, and he appeared with R. Hirsch
before the Court. The judges, however, decided to put
all three under arrest, that is, R. Hirsch, my brother and
R. Ḥayyim. My brother was imprisoned without any cause,
for he did not have any bad coins in his possession; all
his money was of full and tried weight, as was attested
by all the Hungarian nobles with whom he had done
business. However, the judges were of opinion that if
the innocent were never imprisoned it would not be pos-

---

[1] Township in Galicia at the famous pass of the Carpathian mountains.

sible to find out the guilty; and the whole three remained
in prison for a year. For this R. Ḥayyim was most
responsible, as he had a great quantity of this bad money.
With great difficulty, and by dint of tireless efforts and
many intercessions, they were released from prison on the
admission and attestation of the friars of the Bernardine
Monastery that all the faulty money which had been
found in the possession of R. Ḥayyim had come from
their Monastery. The monks had collected in the treasury
of the Monastery for many years large quantities of these
golden coins, which had been given to them by the nobles
for charitable works. The nobles had the habit, when a
sum of golden coins reached them, of choosing the full-
weighted ducats to keep in their treasuries, and the bad
and light ones were spent in purchasing goods from
Jewish traders, who were thus deceived as to the value
of the money they took, and also in works of charity
for various monasteries. It was, therefore, difficult to
ascertain from what sources this money came, but it
was mostly circulated by the nobles, who spent it on
pleasure and in card-playing at Warsaw and Lemberg.
During the sittings of the Diets the nobles arranged
banquets and balls, which lasted the whole night, and
spent their time eating, drinking and card-playing, reck-
lessly throwing away great sums of money. They used
the bad coins especially for gambling, taking from
them even the little bit of gold that they contained,
and using it for their weapons and domestic utensils. [1]
Furthermore, the nobles exchanged good coins for bad
ones with Jewish merchants, making a good profit out
of these transactions, and they took the bad coins to the
goldsmiths to have them improved. After this was done
the nobles again circulated the coins among the merchants
as good ones, thus deceiving them. In this way the matter
was cleared up, and R. Ḥayyim of Dukla was released

---

[1] This statement is confirmed by A. Kitowitcz in the first volume of his
Memoirs (P.) Lemberg, 1882. p. 49.

from prison. My brother, who was proved not to have had even one defective ducat, was compensated for his wrongful imprisonment with a sum of 400 Rhenish gulden and other sums.

In the meantime the wines purchased by my brother, Aryeh Loeb, reached Lemberg, together with the wines bought by my partner, and they were all sold by my brother's clerk, Joseph, the son of R. Samuel Lukowtser; and I also did my best to help him in the sale. I was very angry and sad at my brother's bitter misfortune in being kept in prison for a year. As a result of this trouble and the broken heart it caused me, spots appeared on my chest. An expert doctor, who examined me, told me that as the result of the great trouble and anxiety I had experienced my bile had overflowed and given rise to the spots on my skin. The doctor gave me a prescription for a plaster, which cleansed the bile, and I recovered, especially after my brother came out of prison, as it was clearly ascertained that he did not have any forged money on him.

I will now tell of the great advantage that was derived by my brethren, the children of Israel, thanks to my knowledge of the Polish language and writing. Also I will tell how it happened that the excellent Chief Rabbi and President of the *Beth Din* of the Holy Community of Lemberg and the Provinces learnt of my existence. It chanced that there died in 513 (1753) in the town of Komarno, which is near Lemberg, a respected and wealthy person, the *Aluf* R. Aaron, who left his fortune to his sons. There appeared, however, before the Court his son-in-law, R. Samuel, son of R. Jacob, son of R. Fischel, living at Kalusz[1], who presented a deed (*shetar*) by which the deceased father settled upon his daughter half of the share settled upon the sons. The deed was sealed and witnessed by trustworthy witnesses, and was to the effect that the late R. Aaron had promised him 40,000

---

[1] Small town in Eastern Galicia

gulden. The case was brought before the great *Beth Din*
of Lemberg, and both parties, the plaintiff and defendants,
appeared before the *Beth Din* of the Holy Community of
Lemberg and the Provinces, and before the famous Gaon,
Rabbi Ḥayyim Cohen Zedek Rapaport. R. Samuel presented the deed[1] and laid it on the "clear" table of the
Beth Din, so that the Rabbis might investigate it thoroughly
and test the genuineness of the seal. The heirs of the
deceased claimed against their brother-in-law, Samuel,
that this *shetar* was forged. They declared that their late
father had never made a deed concerning such a large
sum, and that the deed was clearly a forgery, seeing that
the whole property left did not amount to 40,000 gulden,
and that possibly the whole of their father's fortune
during his life had never reached such a sum. The judges,
at the head of whom was the President of the *Beth Din*,
the Gaon Ḥayyim Cohen Zedek Rapaport, asked to be
furnished with letters signed by the witnesses, whose
signatures were on the aforesaid *shetar* written at Komarno,
and there were presented many letters. The judges
examined all the letters and compared them clossly, but
could not find any difference in the writing of the *shetar*.
The claim of the defendants, the heirs, was therefore not
proved, and the *shetar* was found valid. In view, however, of
the strong arguments of the defendants, judgment was given
by the Gaon and the *Beth Din* that the plaintiff R. Samuel
should swear as to the righteousness of his claim by the
oath of the Torah, a very solemn oath; this was imposed on
him by the judges in order to pacify the defendants. Also
his wife was ordered to be present in the synagogue to listen
to the oath and to corroborate it with the response "Amen".
After this oath had been taken the sons of the deceased
were to be obliged to pay the whole sum mentioned in the
shetar, that is, 40,000 gulden, to be realized out of the choicest
of the property left by their late father, R. Aaron.

---

[1] A specimen of this kind of *shetar*, with explanatory notes, is given by
Samuel ben David Halevi in his *Naḥlath Shibah*, Fürth.

This verdict was signed and sealed by the President and his court, and handed to R. Samuel. However, as his wife refused to be present in the synagogue and to listen to the oath of her husband and to respond with "Amen", for that would do a great wrong to her brothers, her husband, R. Samuel, was obliged to arbitrate and to agree to settle his claim by compromise. Both parties chose two judges each, and the President of the *Beth Din* of Lemberg and the Provinces was selected by both parties to be the fifth judge; there was, therefore, what is called in Latin a *super-arbiter*. Both parties appeared before their chosen judges and declared beforehand that they would agree to whatever judgment might be given and abide by it. Both parties gave this undertaking willingly, signed and sealed it, and withdrew their claims and handed them to the *Beth Din*, — as has always been the custom in cases of compromise for many years. The verdict given by the chosen Rabbis was as follows: that if the heirs would desist from their demand for an oath of the *Torah*, they should hand to R. Samuel, in exchange for the *shetar*, 10,000 gulden. This verdict was signed, and the first verdict concerning the 40,000 gulden was declared null and void.

R. Samuel reported to his father, R. Jacob, son of R. Fischel, who lived at Kalusz, all about this affair, and tried to slander the Gaon, saying that for the first verdict he had accepted a bribe of 40 ducats from his hands, and for the second verdict he had been paid with 10 ducats from the other side. The father of R. Samuel was very angry that his son had lost 30,000 gulden through the President of the *Beth Din*.

Subsequently there arrived at Kalusz Cieszkowski, chief steward of all the estates of the Prince Czartoryski, the Voyevoda of the Province of Red Ruthenia, and Governor of Lemberg and its district.[1] R. Jacob, son of R. Fischel,

---

[1] Prince August Alexandre Czartoryski occupied this position from 1731. The Voyevoda exercised special jurisdiction over the Jews. See Introduction, p. 35.

laid before the steward a grave charge against the President
of the *Beth Din*, accusing him of perverting justice and
receiving bribes from both parties concerned. R. Jacob
explained to the steward that the Rabbi had delivered a
verdict in accordance with the Law, whereby his son,
R. Samuel, was to receive 40,000 gulden, the Rabbi having
been bribed with 40 ducats. Later the Rabbi had given a
verdict by which his son, R. Samuel, had received only
10,000 gulden, the Rabbi accepting a bribe from the defendants to the amount of 10 ducats. "Was such a thing
ever heard of before", he said, "that a Rabbi and President of a *Beth Din* should do such a great wrong, and
that my son should lose because of him the large sum
of 30,000 gulden?" He added many more slanders against
the Rabbi and the *Beth Din*, with the result that the
steward was greatly incensed, and declared that such
a thing was unheard-of in all the courts of justice in
the world.

The post of Rabbi at Kalusz was then held by the
son[1] of R. Judah Loeb, President of the Talmudic Academy of Lemberg, and grandson of R. Ḥayyim Cohen
Rapaport. The Rabbi, who was still a young man, was
summoned to appear before the steward, who, after pour-
ing abuse on the Rabbi's grandfather, said with much
heat: "Has such a thing ever happened before in any
nation of the world, that in one lawsuit two verdicts should
be given, one contradicting the other? After receiving
from one side a bribe of 40 ducats, your grandfather
accepted from the other side a smaller bribe of 10 ducats,
to make his first verdict null and void. Neither God nor
man can bear such a wrong. Therefore, tell your grandfather this. Up to this day I have been his friend and
trusted all his words and deeds, since the time he was
made a Rabbi. I presented him to the Prince, the *Voyevoda*,
and I succeeded in obtaining the letter of appointment.

---

[1] The name is omitted. Perhaps R. Dob Berish Rapaport, Rabbi at
Medzyboz. See Buber, *op. cit.*, p. 42.

I have kept him in his position with all my energy and influence for twenty years,[1] and although I have heard of charges made against him by several Jews,[2] I have not believed them, but have regarded them as baseless calumnies prompted by the envy of his enemies. I have kept him in his position because he is an elderly man of upright character and acknowledged and loved by the majority of Israel. Now, however, that his real worthlessness is revealed, I see that he has done many injustices during the time he has held office, and that all the charges brought against him are true. Therefore, there is no other way for him but to quit Lemberg before I arrive there, to escape the severe punishment which I shall be forced to inflict on him. Do not regard my words as idle threats. As you are his grandson, write to him quickly, that should I find him at Lemberg he will be sorry for it, as I shall feel obliged to pass on him a judgment that befits a judge who perverts justice."

Just then it happened that there appeared before the steward a Jew from Skole, R. Jacob, son of R. Loeb Klimtser, to ask for his seal to confirm a verdict passed by the President of the *Beth Din* of Lemberg against a Jew, an inhabitant of Skole. When R. Jacob saw and heard with what contempt the steward spoke against the President of the *Beth Din* of Lemberg, he decided not to produce the verdict he had brought, being afraid that the nobleman might tear it up in his rage. So he went away, and advised the Rabbi of Kalusz not to stay any longer with the steward. "If", he said, "you wish to write a letter and to send it to your venerable grandfather, I will wait until the letter is written and will hand it directly to him." The Rabbi asked him to wait

---

[1] Ḥayyim Rapaport was Rabbi at Lemberg from 1741 (see Buber, *op. cit.* p. 69), whilst this story happened in 1753. "Twenty" must be a slip of the author's pen.

[2] The records of the Court of the Voyevoda at Lemberg contain two charges brought before this court against R. Ḥayyim Rapaport. See the publication of Z. Pazdro, quoted on p. 1, documents NN 25 and 30.

a little, and wrote a letter to his grandfather, in which he informed the latter that the steward was angry with him because it was alleged that he had taken bribes from the two parties to a suit and had given two contradictory verdicts in one case.

R. Jacob went to Lemberg and handed the letter at once to the Rabbi, who was greatly perturbed, and said: "If I could only find some one who writes Polish well I could explain to the steward the whole affair of this lawsuit. He would have the sense to know that I surely did right in this case, and what a benefit I conferred on the son of the man who now denounces me." R. Jacob replied: "I know a man who is a Jew and who writes Polish as nobody else can. All the nobles are astonished that he writes so well, and praise him for his fluency in the Polish language. It is only a pity that it is impossible to bring him here; he is engaged all day selling wine in his wine shop, and cannot leave his business even for an hour. He is the young R. Ber, the brother of the well-known *Kazin* R. Aryeh Loeb of Bolechow." The Rabbi replied: "I myself know the Polish language a little, but not perfectly; and when a Gentile writes for me he never expresses my meaning properly. The only thing for me to do is to write what I want to say myself in Polish on a clean sheet of paper; then if you will kindly go to R. Ber and ask him to put the substance of it in other words, I will look at both copies and send to the steward the one which pleases me better." The Rabbi then sent for R. Isaac, who at that time was the *Shtadlan* of the Council of Four Lands in Poland,[1] and ordered him to copy from his minutes both verdicts; namely, the first sentence passed in accordance with the Jewish Law, that if the plaintiff took the oath, he would receive 40,000 gulden, and the second based on a decision of judges

---

[1] Council or *Vaad* of Four Lands is the usual name of the supreme representative body of the Jews in Poland. See Introduction, p. 34, 36. The *Shtadlan* (advocate) was one of the chief executive officers appointed by the Council, and was a very influential person, sometimes the real leader of the whole of Polish Jewry.

chosen by both parties, that he would receive 10,000 gulden without taking any oath. The Rabbi finished the letter and gave it to R. Jacob, who left with it. The Rabbi then proceeded to the synagogue, and said his afternoon prayers with his usual devotion. Afterwards he brought the letter to me, before dark, and asked me in the name of the Rabbi to read it and to write it afresh. He gave me some sheets of very handsome heavy foolscap paper, and asked me to correct the mistakes and to rewrite his letter in my own handwriting, relying on my thorough knowledge of the Polish language. After reading the whole document I saw that the Rabbi had a perfectly good case, and that the accusations of his detractors were the mendacious calumnies of some ignorant person who did not understand legal procedure.

In the middle of the night I took my pen and set out the Rabbi's case in a letter to the chief steward of the Prince, putting it in scholarly Polish, such as is used in legal affairs, and explaining fully how both verdicts came to be rendered. I also had to write out afresh the verdicts given by the Rabbi, as they were full of errors and written in a style foreign to the Polish language. I then put the three documents in an envelope and wrote thereon all the titles of the steward. In the morning R. Jacob came to fetch the letter from me for the Rabbi, who, after reading it through, said to his wife, "Blessed be the Lord that His Loving-kindness has not left me. I trust to the compassion of Heaven that when the steward sees this letter he will surely recognise and admit that I did right in this case, and that the people who libel me are lying and do not understand legal procedure." A Jew who knew how to ride a horse was fetched at once, and the Rabbi wrapped the letter together with the copies of the verdicts into one envelope and handed them to this messenger. The letter reached the steward in the town of Brzezan,[1] and after reading it he understood at once that the Rabbi's expla-

---

[1] In Eastern Galicia.

nations were correct, and that the assertions of his calum-
niators were malicious lies, and denunciations of God
and His Holy Law. The two contradictory verdicts in this
one case were quite right, for such was the usual procedure
in lawsuits. The first verdict, based on the *Torah*, required
the taking of an oath, which was regarded as a hardship;
and so the suitors preferred to arrive at a compromise.
Hence the second verdict, by which the plaintiff accepted
less without taking the solemn oath, because his wife did
not want to share the oath with him and to respond "Amen"
against her brothers, the heirs; so that Samuel and his
wife were themselves responsible for their great loss.

After Poniatowski had been appointed Commander-in-
Chief[1] he sent people to Danzig and to the Fairs of Leipzig,
which is in Saxony, ordering them to bring thence many
articles, namely, clothes, materials, gold and silver watches,
snuff boxes and other valuables, such as gold and jewelled
rings. On these purchases he spent great sums of money.
With all these things he intended to bribe the gentry, that is,
the *Szlachta*, to win their favour, that they might support him
in political affairs, which were being discussed in the chief
provincial towns. There, in the towns where the Court of
the Starosta[2] sat, dietines[3] of all the nobles met in order to
elect by general consent able and trustworthy men of their
order, to be sent as deputies to the Diet at Warsaw.

Of even more importance than all these presents was
the desire of Poniatowski to obtain good wine to entertain the distinguished nobles. It happened that when
Poniatowski was at Stryi, there lived there a Jew, the
late Saul Wal,[4] who was a very exceptional man, possessed

---

[1] See p. 52.

[2] Court of the nobility in criminal cases and in certain civil cases if one
of the parties was a non-resident noble.

[3] Local diets, in Polish: *Sejmiki*.

[4] Here and throughout the rest of this translation the phrase "be his
memory for a blessing", which in Hebrew is commonly appended to the
name of a dead person, is omitted.

of great ability and profound scholarship, devoted to the welfare of his fellow-Jews, and accustomed to plead their cause before the nobles, by whom he was very greatly respected. Our father was related to Saul on the side of his mother, who was named Braina: Saul's wife, Pessil, was my father's aunt, the sister of his grandfather Jacob.[1] Saul was engaged in leasing estates from the nobles and cultivating these estates with the help of the serfs. This had been his occupation from his youth. The town of Stryi, with all the surrounding villages, was leased by Saul for many years. Count Poniatowski, when appointed to the position of Starosta of the town of Stryi, became acquainted with Saul, and soon discovered that he was a man of great sagacity, so that he always consulted him.

Once Poniatowski said to Saul: "I should like to send someone to Hungary to buy me a considerable quantity of good wine. If you know of a fellow-Jew, a trustworthy person who understands the business, I will send him." Saul replied: "I know a Jew who understands the wine business as no one else does; he speaks Hungarian perfectly, and he has been versed from his youth in the Hungarian wine trade." R. Saul sent at once for my father and introduced him to Poniatowski, who was favourably impressed. He accordingly decided to send my father for the wine, and handed him 2,000 ducats, that is, 36,000 gulden.[2] He also sent with my father the tutor of his sons, in the capacity of a clerk, in order to register the purchase of the wines and the daily expenses, so that a proper account might be kept. The clerk was named Kostiushko.[3] My father did as he was requested by Poniatowski. He bought 200 casks of Tokay wine of the variety called *máslás*.[4] When they both returned from Hungary and brought the wines to Stryi, Poniatowski was very pleased with the purchase; he gave my father 100 ducats for his

[1] Apparently the father of Braina.
[2] See Introduction, p. 26.
[3] Kościuszko?
[4] See note on p. 55.

trouble, and for keeping the accounts properly the clerk Kostiushko was promoted to be steward of our native town Bolechow, and he governed our town for many years.

R. Saul also received a great reward from this business. From his youth he had been, as I have said, a tenant engaged in the leasing of estates, and had been well versed in all kinds of agricultural work and in cattle-breeding. He held for many years leases of the town of Skole with its villages, and also of the Starostaship of Stryi with the surrounding localities. From this occupation he made enough to keep himself and his family in comfort. He had ten fine sons and one daughter. All his children married into families of Rabbis and other notable people. But after Poniatowski had become the Starosta of Stryi he did not wish to sell the town in lease to anyone, but kept it under his own administration through his officials. Thus R. Saul was deprived of his living in his old age, and was unable to meet his obligations to certain nobles, to whom he was indebted. My father advised him to take up his own business, the Hungarian wine trade; and R. Saul followed the advice of my father, and went with him to Hungary. He bought wines, brought them back, and sold them at a good profit, which put him in a position to satisfy all his creditors.

My father worked hard at his trade in partnership with my elder brother, Aryeh Loeb. Every year they travelled to Hungary on horses, and brought from there wine for the nobles living in their neighbourhood. My brother lived with his wife Rachel in the house of my father, in the new apartments which were constructed by my father on the side of the northern gate for the accommodation of passing travellers.[1]

In 489 (1729) there was a fire at Bolechow, and five large buildings situated in the main street of the town were burnt to the ground. One of the houses, which belonged to R. Judah, the son of R. Eliezer, has been rebuilt, and now belongs to R. Michael, the son of R. Abra-

---

[1] Ber's father was inn-keeper. See Introduction, p. 4.

ham. The second house belonged to R. David, the son of
R. Eber[1] Kaz, and now belongs to R. Saul. The third
building belonged to R. Ber, the son of the *Kazin* R. Joseph,
and on the same spot there now stands the house of
R. Meir, son of Ber Cohen, and of his brother Eber. The
fourth was owned by R. Manes, and is now the property
of his grandsons. The fifth was the property of the widow
Sprinza, the wife of R. Israel, son of Leah,[2] and the present
building standing on this site belongs to my son, R. Joseph.[3]
On the northern side of that house there was a plot of
waste ground belonging to R. Reuben, whereby the fire
was prevented from spreading, and it was for this reason
that the rest of the buildings in that street were saved.
The five houses mentioned were totally destroyed, together with the outhouses at the back of them. A woman
named Ziril Kremrin, a shopkeeper, perished in the conflagration.

In the year . . .[4] during the Feast of the Epiphany,
which fell on a Friday, after the Gentiles had left the
church, a lighted candle fell on a table covered with a
silken cloth and caused a great fire in the whole of the
building, a construction of thick oak. After the fire had
consumed the inner part of the church, a priest happened
to open a door; the flames leapt out of the doorway and
burnt the rest of the building. The church was utterly
demolished by the time of the afternoon prayers, on the
eve of Sabbath *Shirah*.[5]

On the same Friday the famous precentor, R. Yekele,
visited our community and read the prayers in our synagogue.

[1] A rather unusual name.

[2] In cases where the mother was for one reason or another more widely
known than the father, it was the name of the mother, not of the father
which was added to that of the child.

[3] Here and throughout this translation the phrase "may his light shine",
which in Hebrew is often appended to the name of a person still living,
is omitted.

[4] The year is omitted in the Manuscript.

[5] Por. Ex. XIII, 17—XVII, 16.

Shortly after that, in the year ...[1] other houses situated
in the main street of the town were destroyed by a fire,
which originated at the house of R. Elimelech Cohen
Zedek, on the site of which now stands a house belonging
to R. Saul Wal.[2] Together with this another house was
destroyed, belonging to the President of the *Beth Din*,
R. Yukel Hurwitz Segal, who then lived there. This house
was situated on the site of the old *Beth Ha-Midrash*.[3] The
fire also destroyed the building of the Gentile Bublik, on
the site of which now stands the house of R. Judah, son of
R. Samuel, who is also known by the name of *Katzshor*.
In the vicinity stood the house of the widow Malka, wife
of the late R. Eliah, the Blind; in our time R. Judah, son
of R. Ḥayyim Auerbach, owns a house on that spot. Near
there the house of Bunam, son of Sheina, was destroyed;
the house now on the site is that of the widow Lipka,
wife of R. Eliah, son of R. Ber. Further along the house
of R. Abraham Dakhiles was totally destroyed, and the
ground is now the site of the house of R. Abraham, son
of R. Simel. Near there the residence of R. Kalman Cohen
Zedek was burnt to the ground; standing in its place is
now the house of his grandson, R. Joseph Hirsch, son of
R. Loeb. The next house destroyed was that of R. Yekele,
whose son-in-law was R. Itamar, a skilful *Mohel*[4]: on its
site stands now the house of R. Loeb, son of R. Joseph,
son of R. Seinwel. The Gentile Onufry also lost his house,
which had already suffered during the first fire, having had
the roof burnt, as it was close to the building where the
previous fire had broken out. On the second occasion it
was utterly destroyed. The fire died out of itself, having
reached the gap caused by the previous conflagration.

My father was steadily pursuing his wine business in
partnership with my elder brother, the late R. Aryeh Loeb.
They travelled to Hungary every year to purchase wines

---

[1] The year is omitted in the manuscript.
[2] Probably a descendant of the Saul Wal mentioned above.
[3] House of Study, belonging to the community.
[4] A person who performs the ceremony of circumcision.

to sell to the nobles of the vicinity. My brother, Aryeh
Loeb, lived with his wife, Rachel, in my father's house,
but after the fire my brother bought the ground on which
had stood the property of the above-named R. Israel, son
of Leah, and built a large and handsome mansion, far exceed-
ing for size and beauty any other in our town of Bolechow.
There he built a cellar walled with stone, with a large
arched roof, where a hundred casks of wine could be
stored. It is preserved to this day, in the house of my
son, the learned R. Joseph. The building was finished in
497 (1737), as can be seen from the date carved on the
lintel of the stone let in above the iron door which is the
entrance to this cellar.

In the same year — 497 (1737) — on the 6th of the
month of the Second Adar, which fell on a Sabbath
(9th March), my mother, the virtous and pious Esther,
daughter of R. Mordechai, died at 9 o'clock in the evening.
She died in the 54th year of her life, after having been
greatly afflicted for more than a year with dropsy of the
leg. She passed away peacefully, without struggle. At
the same hour and day, on the same date of the month
of Adar (which fell on the 13th March, 1723), my mother
Esther had brought me into the world with great pains
of childbirth, as I narrated on page ...[1] She almost died
in giving birth to me; but out of the compassion of Heaven
on me, the weak and newly-born, there were added to her
life fourteen years more, so that she could bring me up
to obey the *Torah* and the commandments and to bind
the phylacteries.[2]

Let us now return to the narration of what was happening
in our community of Bolechow. Some were of opinion
that the two fires were caused by the troops then stationed
at Bolechow to the number of three regiments. The landlord of the town, Poniatowski, who was then Commander-

---

[1] Not preserved in the Manuscript.

[2] Small leather boxes containing Hebrew texts on vellum, worn by Jews
during the morning prayers on week days to remind them to keep the Law.
The custom is based on Exodus 13, 16.

in-Chief of all the military forces of Poland, called up troops to his estates and paid them largely in cash. The payments were made weekly, and the soldiers spent their money on food and drink.

After the death of the King of Poland and Elector of Saxony, Augustus I,[1] great dissension arose among the Polish nobility. Some of them elected as King the son of the late King, but the majority wanted to place on the throne Leszczynski, a Polish noble who had previously been elected before the late King was crowned, and who would have been enthroned then, with the support of the King of Sweden, had not a compromise been arranged, by which the late King Augustus was allowed to rule over Poland for a certain time, at the expiration of which he declared that he would leave the realm of Poland of his own accord and cede the crown to Leszczynski. The documents referring to that arrangement were preserved by the King of Sweden, Charles XII, and Count Poniatowski, who was present at his death-bed, obtained possession of them by a stratagem. (Some people said that after the death of the King of Sweden, his widow, the Queen, handed the papers to Poniatowski.) The Count immediately went to Augustus II and gave him the documents. Augustus therefore kept the Crown, and did not fulfil his promise to cede it to Leszczynski, but continued to reign himself, as he desired to do.[2] The King promoted Count Ponia-

---

[1] Augustus II, as pointed out before. See footnote on p. 52.

[2] This account, though in the main correct and lucid, contains some erroneous statements. The "compromise" of which Ber speaks was the act of abdication signed by Augustus II in the Peace Treaty of Altranstaedt on the 24th November, 1706. According to this instrument Augustus was to resign ln favour of Leszczynski and only to keep the title of King. Poniatowski was not present at the death of Charles XII. Ulrike Leonore followed her brother Charles XII, who was never married. Our author, who does not quote any authorities, apparently got his information about this eventful period of Polish history from his father. — See Szujski, *History of Poland* (P.), IV, p. 212; Kantecki, *Stanislaus Poniatowski* (P.), 1880, p. 75 and 81, also annotation N. 111; *Souvenirs du Prince Stanislas Poniatowski*, in *Revue d'Histoire Diplomatique*, 1895.

towski and greatly advanced him, as I briefly mentioned above. This displeased the other nobles,[1] who envied Poniatowski and hated him bitterly. But he skilfully contrived to surround himself with many friends, some of whom he made through liberal gifts, and some through flattery.

In the meantime King Augustus died. Many of the nobles took counsel together, and called Leszczynski back from France, telling him that now it would be possible to place him on the Polish throne. But meanwhile the Muscovites, that is, the Russians, entered Poland with the purpose of helping the Elector of Saxony, Augustus, the son of the late King, to instal himself in his father's place. All the nobles who were against Augustus met together in their dietines in the district of Lemberg and in the neighbouring provinces, in order to discuss how to render impossibie the crowning of the Elector of Saxony. They had, however, to retire before the Muscovite troops,[2] who put the nobles to flight, pushing them back through all the towns situated near the frontiers of Hungary. The nobles passed through our town of Bolechow, and, as soon as they learned that it was on the estate of Poniatowski, they designed to rob and pillage the town in order to defray their expenses.[3]

[1] See Barącz, *Memoir of Polish History* (P.), 1856, p. 187; R. Roepell, *Polen um die Mitte des XVIII. Jahrhunderts*, 1876, p. 34.

[2] The author even in his declining years retained the impression made by the sad reminiscences of his youth. Very little is known about the events of those days. I have found valuable information in the priest Barącz's monographs *Pamiątki miasta Stanisławowa* (1858) and *Wolne miasto handlowe Brody* (1865), and also in his collection of rare documents, letters and chronicles, entitled *Pamiętnik dziejów Polskich* (1855). Ber's report is a further source of information on the upheaval in Poland after the death of King Augustus II.

[3] The author does not explain why the Polish nobles in their flight before the Russians intended to pillage the estates of Poniatowski, who for some time was on the side of Leszczynski, but very soon, as Augustus III gained the upper hand, left the former and went over to the new king's party. It was probably for that treachery that the partisans of Leszczynski were eager to revenge themselves on Poniatowski. The province of Red

The Lord gave my father favour in the eyes of all the nobles, thanks to his ability as a pleader and his knowledge of the Polish language, which he had learnt from his youth, and of political affairs. He intervened on behalf of the people, so that none of the nobles incited his fellows to cause any damage to our town, and they left Bolechow as they came, without committing any act of violence and without carrying off any booty. In the other townships of our vicinity, however, the communities suffered great damage and loss. The Lord always remembered my father for the great benefits he had rendered to the people of Bolechow, but the people themselves did not remember their benefactor, but forgot him.

At that time a general called Boreika[1] set out at the head of a large force. At Stryi it was related to him that there lived in Bolechow a Rabbi, who was President of the *Beth Din* and a very rich man, and he made up his mind to confiscate all the property of the Rabbi. This came to the knowledge of the Rabbi, the venerable R. Yukel Segal, on the eve of the Day of Atonement, and on that day after morning prayers I saw with my own eyes the Rabbi mounting a horse to flee to the town of Dolina for safety. But when the general entered Bolechow with his troops he consulted my father, who convinced him that the Jews did not possess large fortunes, and that the Gentiles envied them without reason. The general enquired no further about the Rabbi, and went away from here peacefully.

After the fires which occurred at Bolechow the Rabbi, with his own money, built a handsome and comfortable

Ruthenia, which corresponds more or less to Eastern Galicia, was invaded in 1735 by Russian troops from the direction of the Ukraine, led by the Generals Prince Ludwig Hessen-Homburg and Keith. The Russians entered Brody, Lemberg, Tarnopol and other towns. The population was terrified and lived in fear of excesses. See Barącz, *Memoir of Polish History* (P.), pp. 193—194; L. Rzewuski, *The Chronicle of Podhorce* (P.), 1861, pp. 134—135; Szujski, *op. cit.*, vol. IV, p. 308.

[1] I cannot trace whether he was a Russian general, the libraries and archives in Russia not being at the moment accessible. The name Boreika does not appear in any of the Russian works consulted in the British Museum Library.

house. Shortly after the building was finished the excellent
man was taken from us and appointed to be Rabbi and
President of the *Beth Din* at Brody. In 495 (1735) he was
promoted to the rabbinical seat in the community of Brody.
On his departure all the members of our community, the
young and the aged, came to bid him farewell. With us
went our teacher, the learned R. Elieser Liber, and we,
his pupils, followed him. Before taking his seat in his
carriage the Rabbi addressed the whole people in the
following terms: "Our Sages said in the Talmud, that
one should not take leave of his friends without the
words of the *Halakhah* on his lips.[1] I will therefore explain
to you in a jocular manner some sentences of the *Gemara*.
We have the following verse in the Treatise *Taanith*:
"Care promotes the study of the Law".[2] Rashi explains
"care" as meaning anxiety about earning a living. But
we may ask, why does Rashi give this explanation, when
there are other griefs than anxiety about earning a living?
There is a biblical sentence which runs "And thy life shall
hang in doubt before thee".[3] This refers, as the Talmud
explains, to people who get their bread from the baker's
shop;[4] and the Talmud adds: "Everyone is obliged to
provide food for his family for three years". But it also
says: "Those who ask: What shall we eat tomorrow? are
of little faith"; but everyone has to say daily: Blessed be
the Lord every day. For an explanation of this apparent
contradiction we may quote two other sayings of the
Sages which similarly appear to contradict each other.
"If", they said, "a hen crows like a cock, against nature,
the hen must be killed." But they also said: "It is forbidden to say: Kill this hen, which has crowed like a
cock". The contradiction is only apparent. One may not
say "kill this hen", but the hen must be killed. Similarly,
one is forbidden to *ask*: "What shall we eat tomorrow"?

[1] Ber. 31 a.
[2] S. also Sanh. 26 b.
[3] Deut. 28,66.
[4] Y. Shab. VII, 11a.

but one must provide food for his household. Now it is
written in Proverbs: "If one has heaviness in his heart,
let him communicate his troubles to others"[1], and so be
relieved; but he who has no livelihood is forbidden to
communicate his sorrow to other people by asking: "What
shall we eat tomorrow"? He has, however, to take care
to secure a livelihood for his family. Rashi, then, was
perfectly right in his explanation of the saying: "Care
promotes the study of the Law", because one observes
a precept of the Law by not talking to others about one's
lack of a livelihood, and therefore that particular care
promotes the study of the Law."

After the Rabbi had ended his address, he turned to
my father and said: "R. Judah, you are going to travel
to Hungary; I would ask you to show me a kindness
and to buy me a barrel of good *máslás*". He gave my
father the money for it — 8 ducats, — and added: "I will
try, with the help of God, to find for your son a suitable
wife at Brody from among the daughters of the best
families; he must, however, go on with his studies". All
this I heard from his holy mouth, and I saw him with
my own eyes. The Rabbi then departed. Our teacher
took us back to his house and asked if we had kept the
Rabbi's speech in our minds; and he repeated all that the
Rabbi had said. After this the words were engraved for
ever in the memory of many of my fellow-students, who,
together with me, heard them from the Gaon.

Before Rabbi Yukel Segal had left, his son, R. Mordechai Segal, was appointed to be Rabbi at Bolechow in
his father's place, with the approval of all the members
of the community and in accordance with the will of the
whole Jewish population. The new Rabbi pleased everybody, because he was beyond all doubt a righteous man.
I was then a boy of twelve. My father received two
letters from Rabbi Yukel on the subject of a good match
for me in Brody, and as a consequence I had to visit

[1] Prov. 12,25. The meaning is perverted by a play on words.

R. Mordechai every Saturday after the midday meal and read *Gemara* with him, in order that I might become familiar with Talmudic disputation and law. The Rabbi's sister, the virtuous Leah, renowned for her learning, was living in the house, where she remained after her parents had departed for Brody. She was married to the learned R. Arych Lœb, son of the Rabbi of Dobromil. Rabbi Mordechai used to point out to me the passage I was to read, and then took his afternoon sleep; he was of a delicate constitution all his life. His sister Leah, sitting by us, looked on and saw that I did not understand the passages from the *Gemara* and the commentaries of Rashi. She would say to me: "Why are you puzzled? Tell me the text of the *Gemara* over which you are in doubt". So I would read to her the difficult passage in the *Gemara* or in Rashi's commentary on it, and she would repeat the passage correctly from memory and explain it to me. Thus assisted by her I was able, when the Rabbi awoke, to read the passage aright. This continued during a whole year, so long R. Mordechai lived. For our many sins the illness of the Rabbi became more serious, and he died in 496 (1736). The community decreed a week's mourning and lamentations, and they honoured his memory by not appointing for the space of one year and more another Rabbi in his stead. His widow, the daughter of the Rabbi[1] of Sniatyn, remained for a whole year at Bolechow, receiving the revenues of the Rabbinate, and she went away to her father only after the year of mourning had come to an end.

The next Rabbi at Bolechow was Moses, son of R. Aaron Segal. His eldest brother, R. Mordechai, was the son-in-law of R. Kalman, Elder of the Council of Four Lands, a native of Tysmienica. The younger brother of the new Rabbi[2] at Bolechow occupied the Rabbinical chair at Olesko.[3] After R. Moses had resigned the position at

---

[1] Name omitted in the MS.
[2] Name omitted in the MS.
[3] Olesko is a township, near Brody, in Eastern Galicia.

Bolechow, he became Rabbi at Olesko, whilst his brother, his predecessor at the latter place, moved to Brody, where he survived his elder brother for many years, until the accession to the throne of our Lord the Emperor Joseph II. Later he was made Chief Rabbi of the district of Brody, though during the whole time he lived at Lemberg.

R. Moses, who was Rabbi at Bolechow for ten years, enjoyed great respect, for he carried out his duties with wisdom, in face of the opposition of some leading people of the community. Then he left us with the two sons borne to him by his wife, the daughter of the Rabbi of Stryi, R. Berish, son of R. Moses Ḥarif.[1] These two boys grew up at Bolechow.

In 499 (1739) I was married to a young girl who did not prove to be my destined wife. R. Moses Segal performed the sacred ceremony. This ill-assorted match was due to our great sins. I was forced into this marriage, which was arranged by my stepmother Feige. I lived with my wife for two and a half years, but we had no children, and by the loving-kindness of God, be He praised, I divorced her. And behold, through the providence of His name, be He praised, I was given the right wife who was predestined for me from eternity, after having spent the time as a "widower" in my father's house. I conducted myself as a God-fearing man, attending every morning and evening the service of the synagogue and praying with great devotion. I was deeply engaged in studying the Bible, the *Mishnah*, the *Gemara* and the laws of the *Shulchan Aruch*, besides other ethical works. As a rule I hastened to become acquainted with every book which came to my hand, and to understand the meaning of the author. I learned also the Polish language to please my father, who wanted me to know it. He kept a tutor in his house, an educated Polish gentleman,

---

[1] In the biographical note on Moses Ḥarif in Buber's work, *Anshé Shem*, (H), p. 160, only two sons are named, and no mention is made of R. Berish, the Rabbi of Stryi.

who made me conversant with Polish speech and writing.
I learned it perfectly in a very short time. Moreover, I
studied Latin and understood the principal part of its
grammar. After my first wife left, some of the people in
our community began to gossip about me and to suspect
my faith, saying that I learned these things, God forbid,
not for God's sake, and I had to give up my secular
studies. I occupied myself then entirely with the study
of our Holy *Torah*.

During this time I was often approached with good
offers of marriage. Also, when my father went to Lemberg looking for customers, with samples of wine which
he had stored at Bolechow in considerable quantities, he
took me with him, saying: "Perhaps you will find a good
match there". However, none of the offers made to me
there proved to be suitable. An Armenian[1] wine merchant
named Ribesina, well-known at Lemberg, travelled with
us. He purchased many barrels of excellent wine from
my father to the amount of several hundred ducats, so that
my father did not go without profit to Lemberg; but I
still remained single. Then it happened on the day of Shu-
shan Purim that a lady named Yenta, the wife of R. Isaac
Reischer, the chief of the community of Tysmienica, was
passing on her way through Bolechow and came to stay
in my father's house. She saw me, and said to my sister
Blima: "Well, I have a wonderful match for your brother.
She is beautiful, clever, accomplished and of good family;
her brothers are distinguished scholars". I had already
met this lady, who was a widow, when I stayed with my
father the previous summer at Tysmienica for the Sabbath
Naḥmu, in 5499 (the 15th of August 1739). The day after,
on Sunday (the 16th), my future brother-in-law, R. Meshulam Salman, went with my father to see the landlord of

---

[1] The author usually calls the Armenians "Amalekites"; in this case
however, he uses the word מחה, which occurs in the phrase; "For I will
utterly *put out* the remembrance of Amalek from under Heaven" (Ex. 17,14).
It is not generally known that the Armenian Church in Brody was called
among the Jews *Muchischer Kloister.*

the town in his castle and to show him samples of wine.
My father, having been acquainted with R. Meshulam
Salman for some time, was invited to his house for a cup
of coffee. I also accompanied them, and there I saw the
host's sister, Leah, a very handsome widow. The time was
then ripe for my brother Seeb Wolf to be married, and
my father agreed to the match with this widow, but as
she had a little son by her first husband, it came to nothing.
We both continued our journey through Buczacz and
Czortkow to Kamieniec-Podolsk, where my father sold
many casks of wine for several hundreds of ducats. The
Armenian wine trader arrived later on in Bolechow to
fetch the wines he had bought and to pay the balance.

But we must return to our subject. When my sister
and my sister-in-law, Rachel, learned of my desire to
marry this widow, they talked to Yenta, so that the
match might soon be made. And so it turned out. On
her return home, Yenta discussed the matter with her
husband, R. Isaac Reisher, who was a close friend of
Leah's brothers, Rabbi Issachar Ber, (who had just returned
from Amsterdam, where he studied the *Torah* with the
Gaon, R. Moses Ḥagiz[1], of the Portuguese community
there), and Meshulam Salman. They both followed the
advice of R. Isaac Reisher and sent a letter written by
him through a special messenger, a Gentile, in which the
hope was expressed that my brothers would come with
me to Tysmienica in order to settle the affair satisfactorily.
On a Sunday, the 27th of the month of Adar, 502 (27th of
March, 1742), we all started for Tysmienica, and arrived
there on the following Tuesday, during the time of afternoon prayer. In the evening the affair was discussed,
and I had to go with them to see Leah before the ceremony of betrothal was performed. The meeting between
both families — my brothers and the brothers of my
future wife — took place in the mansion of the Elder of

---

[1] He was teaching at Amsterdam in the years between 1704—1714. See
Jewish Encyclopedia VI, p. 151.

the Council of Four Lands, R. Mordechai, the son-in-law
of the *Kazin*, R. Kalman, and the brother of R. Moses
Segal, Rabbi of our community of Bolechow. This Rabbi
wrote to R. Mordecai a very effusive letter on the merits
of my brothers, which had the effect of making R. Mordechai throw himself heart and soul into the affair and do
everything possible for our benefit. So it was that he
became the mediator between the parties and that he
received all the monies into his hands. My first *shushbin*[1]
was R. Mordechai's son-in-law, R. Moses (son of R. Joshua
Hurwitz Segal and nephew of R. Yukel Segal, Rabbi
at Brody), and the second R. Schmeril, son of R. Selig,
formerly Rabbi at Tysmienica.

On the eve of Thursday, the first of the month Nissan,
502 (5th of April, 1742), the wedding took place. The
Gaon, R. Monish, Rabbi at Tysmienica (formerly at
Polonnoye[2]) performed the marriage ceremony. My brothers left Tysmienica the day after the wedding, and
returned home to Bolechow to spend the Sabbath there.
I remained with my father-in-law, the learned R. Joshua,
whose house was full of beautiful books, the like of which
is not often seen. He had also fine furniture, large and
handsome cauldrons of copper, and silver and gold vessels,
such as one would expect in a rich man's house. My
money, lent out at interest, was in safe hands. I used
to visit the holy synagogue every morning and evening
and to say my prayers, for it is stated in the *Shulchan
Arukh* that only prayers offered up in the Synagogue are
heard. I devoted a fixed time every day to studying the
Talmud and its commentaries in the *Beth Hamidrash*. My
teacher was R. Isaac, who soon afterwards was appointed
Rabbi at Gwozdziec.[3] Besides him other excellent scholars
living at Tysmienica made friends with me, especially
the learned R. Mordechai, the brother of our Rabbi at

---

[1] A sort of "best man".
[2] Town in Volhynia.
[3] Township in Eastern Galicia, in the district of Kolomea.

Bolechow. I first made a name for myself when, during the Fast of Ab, I carved for my stepson, a boy of six, a wooden sword in the shape of the iron swords of the nobles called "Karabela".[1] During the recital of the lamentations very few people were following the reading, as most of them were taken up in admiring my carving.

It further happened at that time that certain merchants of Breslau sent their representative to Tysmienica with promissory notes of the well-known merchant R. Zebi Hirsch Gabai, amounting to the sum of 25,000 gulden. This German, with the assistance of some Jewish merchants at Tysmienica, made an inventory of the liabilities of R. Hirsch. The affair was settled by compromise. R. Wolf, chief of the community at Stryi, acted for the one side, and for the other the *Parnas*[2] of the community of Tysmienica during that month, Jacob Koppel, the Fat. R. Monish, Rabbi of Tysmienica, was the arbitrator. Judgment was given in the holy language and signed by the arbiters. But just at that time arrived Prince Jablonowski, the landlord of Tysmienica and Starosta of Czyhyryn.[3] The judgment had to be translated into Polish in order to be presented to the Prince; and not a single Jew was to be found who was able to do it. The people learned that I was well versed in the Polish language, so they sent for me to be brought to the *Parnas*, Jacob Koppel. I was placed at a table, where paper, ink and a copy of the decision of the Judge were ready. Near me was seated R. Isaac Reischer, who had arranged my marriage. He saw me reading the judgment in the holy language and putting it into Polish. There were present also the German from Breslau, the creditor of

---

[1] According to W. Lozinski, *Polnisches Leben in vergangenen Zeiten*, Munich, 1918, pp. 190—191, "Karabela" was a fancy sword. A certain nobleman, Karabela, had introduced a light and ornamental sword in 1496 at the Polish Court, being an imitation of the real weapon. The designation "Karabela" became common, however, as late as the eighteenth century.

[2] Member (elder) of the communal hierarchy. See Introduction, p. 35.

[3] Famous town in the Ukraine.

R. Hirsch. My translation was read to them and pleased them. The merchant from Breslau gave me a Rhenish ducat, and R. Koppel gave me seven gulden, that is, half a ducat. The verdict with my Polish translation of it was presented to the Prince, who read my translation and confirmed the verdict by signing it. After this people got to know of my little knowledge, and they began to show me friendship, even the best people, and especially those who were accomplished writers in the holy language, of whom there were many. Foremost among them was a young man, Joseph, the son of Jacob Koppel the Fat, and son-in-law of R. Isaac, Rabbi at Monasteryszcze. He was a wonderful writer in the holy language, and I envied him more than all the other writers. He gave me many of his writings to keep, but they all perished in the fire which broke out in 519 (1759) because of our many sins, as I shall relate in its place.

After my marriage my wife's family induced me to start business by opening a shop with various kinds of merchandise. My own idea was to lend money to Gentiles on the security of their pledges. I became acquainted with this kind of business during the time I spent in the house of my teacher, R. Joseph of Dolina. Mostly it was I who wrote out the amount borrowed on the pledges and the date when the interest began, and it was partly because I was acquainted with money-lending that I felt inclined to take it up, although none of my family before me had been engaged in that business. But my wife and her family were opposed to this idea, and persuaded me to open a shop, which I ran for two years.

In the month of Adar in 503 (1743) a son was born to us, and we called him Joshua, after my deceased father-in-law.

The landlord of the estate of Tysmienica, Prince Jablonowski, then resolved to plunder the inhabitants of the town, as he had obtained it by fraud, and knew that he would have to relinquish it because it was not his inherited estate.

The Jewish merchants of Tysmienica were at that time more famous than those of Brody; and they remained so until the first fire which occurred in the latter place in 1752,[1] after which the landlord of Brody, Count Potocki, the Crown Hetman,[2] advanced his townspeople the sum of a million gulden out of his treasury. The merchants of Brody, having received this sum in cash, immediately found their way to all the towns of Europe where valuable merchandise and merchants were to be found. They also went to the seaports, the centres of foreign trade, and there carried on business with the money lent them by the Prince, for which they paid seven per cent. interest, whilst the capital remained in their hands for many years without loss. In this way the Jews of Brody became foremost in every kind of business, and every place became full of them and of their goods. Their fame continues unto this day, and it will never die out or become less.

And now the landlord of Tysmienica, Prince Jablonowski, came to rob and plunder the people of that town, for a reason which I will explain. This estate was the inheritance of the Prince's brother-in-law, Wielhorski, then still a boy, brought up in the house of his grandmother, who owned the estate of Tysmienica. When this lady died,[3]

---

[1] According to S. Barącz in his monograph on Brody (*Wolne miasto handlowe Brody*, 1865, p. 93) the fire took place on May 6th, 1742, and utterly destroyed several houses and shops, the damage amounting to some millions of gulden. Many people perished in the flames. Ber's date 1752 is a mistake, or possibly a slip of the pen, for he uses the right date later on.

[2] Count Joseph Potocki, one of the most powerful and influential Polish magnates of that time. Potocki's loan to the Jews of Brody is not mentioned in the monograph of Barącz, who only says that the Armenians left Brody after the great fire, whilst the Jews remained and concentrated a widely ramified trade in their hands. Still, Baracz emphasizes the great interest taken in the economic development of Brody by Joseph Potocki (who died in 1751) and by his son Stanislaus, the Voyevoda of Kiev.

[3] According to S. Barącz's monograph on Tysmienica (included in his *Pamiętnik dziejów polskich*, 1855), Countess Johanna Wielhorska died on the 11th of May, 1741, in her 63rd year. "The town", says Barącz, "lost in her a magnanimous lady". — Further, Barącz says that Prince John Kajetan Jablonowski, married to Therese Wielhorska, became the landlord of Tysmienica in 1745.

Prince Jablonowski wanted to become trustee of the boy
Wielhorski, and to hold the estates of the young orphan.
The other members of the family did not, however, agree
that the Prince should be the trustee, whereupon he sent
some of his domestics to kidnap the boy Wielhorski, in
his sleep, from the castle of Tysmienica and to carry him
to the Prince's palace. Thereafter Jablonowski arrived in
Tysmienica with an armed force and forcibly took possession of the estate of the young orphan. The Elders
and Chiefs of the Jewish community were denounced to
the Prince for having requested the relatives of Count
Wielhorski to prevent Jablonowski from becoming the
trustee of the property of Tysmienica; and the Prince
therefore decided to take his revenge on the Jews and
to despoil them of everything possible. He ordered 350
barrels of honey to be brought from his estates in the
Ukraine, (he was then Starosta of Czyhyryn), and as soon as
the barrels reached Tysmienica he ordered the Elders and
and Chiefs of the Jewish community to distribute all the
honey among its members, who had to pay to the treasury
of the Prince, at the end of seven days, 8 ducats for
each barrel of honey. The *Kahal*[1] therefore had to impose
a tax on all the members of the community, each according
to his means. I was taxed to pay for half a barrel of
honey — 4 ducats; and as the barrels could only fetch 6
ducats each, I lost 2 ducats. As a result of this my wife
agreed to move from Tysmienica and to set up our home
in my father's house at Bolechow. We left Tysmienica
on a Tuesday in the week of the Portion *Beshalah*.[2] My
wife Leah and I reached my father's house at Bolechow
on the evening of Friday, the eve of the Sabbath *Beshalah*,
in 504 (27th January 1744), with our first-born son, Joshua,
who was born to us at Tysmienica, and was a beautiful
child. My father and the other members of our family
were happy that we had arrived in safety, and my aged

---

[1] The Board of the community. See Introduction, p. 34.
[2] Portion Ex. XIII, 17 — XVII, 16.

grandfather, R. Hirsch, was especially delighted to see our little boy. He at once took the child in his arms, wept a long time, and said: "The Lord has granted to me also the privilege of beholding his seed";[1] and his eyes streamed with tears of joy.

One month after our arrival my grandfather, R. Hirsch, son of R. Judah Loeb, fell ill, and he passed away on the Sabbath *Terumah*[2] (2nd of February, 1744). When we returned home from the synagogue after the morning service, he blessed us all, laying his hands upon the head of each one; and at the time of afternoon prayers his holy soul left his pure body, gently and without any agony. He had lived to 104 years. He was born in Great Meseritch, near Brest-Litovsk, as I wrote above on page . . ,[3] and at the time of the wars of the Cossack Khmelnitski, (1648), he was a boy of 8 years.

I lived with my wife in my father's house, in the special rooms which were reserved for guests (Jews and Gentiles alike). For the first time I left for Hungary to start a business. I carried with me brandy, herrings, different kinds of spices, wax and other articles needed in the towns and villages throughout the county of Maramaros-Sziget. All these articles I sold for cash, except the brandy, which was sold on several months' credit to a trustworthy person. I also sold the fine horse on which I rode, and gained over this transaction a profit of $3^{1}/_{2}$ ducats, and I returned home in time for the Passover.

Before the Feast of Weeks I sent my messenger, R. Hirsch Nekhis, a grandson of my uncle, to collect the outstanding debts for the brandy which I had left on credit. R. Hirsch made the journey to Hungary together with R. Samuel Abrosis (whose wife was a grand-daughter of my uncle, R. Asriel Selig), and he received the whole sum for the brandy. On their way back they stopped

---

[1] Paraphrase of Gen. 48[11].
[2] Portion Ex. XXV, 1 — XXVII, 19.
[3] Not preserved.

in the village of Budfalu, near the town of Maramaros-Sziget, for the Sabbath. Afterwards, in the evening of the Sabbath, they both went to lie down before the windows in the front of the house. R. Hirsch looked out and noticed in the meadows a fire made by the groom, at which he said: "Why should I lie here on the boards where fleas abound? I had rather go into the meadow to lie down there on the grass and look after my horse which is there". He went; but R. Samuel Abrosis, his companion, remained by himself on his couch before the house door. And behold, there came several night-robbers and found R. Samuel asleep. One of the band raised his axe and hit R. Samuel one blow on the head, chopping off an ear together with a portion of the skull, so that R. Samuel's brain fell right out and he expired at once. Through this murder the host of the inn, R. Jonah Budfaler, was made aware of the coming of the band, and before they succeeded in opening the door, he fled with his wife by way of the roof-chamber of the house. He then alarmed the whole village, causing a rush to his place, whereupon the band of robbers made off. R. Hirsch, having spent the whole night in the meadow, did not know of what had happened; so he was saved from death. The money he had received for the brandy was safe on him.

We in Bolechow knew nothing of this incident. It happened, however, that R. Baruch of the village of Cerkowna[1] invited me to perform the circumcision of his son; and there was present at the feast R. Michel, son of R. Seinwel, a resident of the village of Polanica.[2] During the feast he reported how R. Samuel Abrosis had been murdered by bandits. I felt upset, knowing that R. Samuel was travelling to Hungary with my messenger, R. Hirsch; and as soon as the ceremony was finished I rode from there to Skole through the village of Polanica to ascertain what had happened. I was told that my messenger was

---

[1] In the district of Dolina, in Eastern Galicia.
[2] In the district of Stryi, in Eastern Galicia.

alive and had not lost any of his money. In the
meantime R. Hirsch arrived with the money, and handed
it to me in proper order. Then I understood clearly
that the Providence of the Lord, may His Name be
praised, is with His creatures, and that he had fed me
all my life long. His mercy and the multitude of His
loving kindnesses has preserved us and all our belongings, and He will reward us with the plentitude of His
mercy for ever.

In the same summer I purchased from the landlord of our
neighbourhood prime hides of she-goats and he-goats,
also about 50 bundles of excellent flax. I brought these
goods to Hungary, where they were sold at a good
profit. The hides I sold in the town of Huszt. The flax
was sold at Debreczen, partly for cash and partly in
exchange for lamb-skins, namely the Transylvanian black
skins, thoroughly tanned, which I then carried to Poland.
Some of my fellow-Jews denounced me, saying that I
had tried to evade the payment of the imperial customs
duties. The customs collector therefore came from Stryi
to the village of Volosets, and impounded my goods. I
had to give him two very nice rugs and some other small
things besides to induce him to exempt me from the fine
for smuggling — "contraband", as my father used to say.

Up to this time my father and my brother, Aryeh Loeb,
had been continuously engaged in the Hungarian wine
trade for more than 30 years. During the life time of our
mother, Esther, peace and concord reigned between them,
and even when my father married his second wife, Feige,
they remained on good terms, as I have related above.
But as time went on and year followed year, there arose
conflicts and quarrels between my father's wife and my
brother's wife, Rachel. So my brother sought and found
a rich nobleman desirous of starting business in Hungarian
wines. He gave my brother 800 ducats, and attached to
him a Polish clerk to keep the books of the business. My
brother then departed for Hungary and left my father
behind at home, deprived of the trade in which he had

been thoroughly versed from his early youth. My father was very angry and grieved.

My stepmother, Feige, then approached my wife with a clever suggestion. "You", she said, "have quite a nice sum of money. What is the use of putting it into a precarious trade, where you are likely to lose it? Would it not be better for you, at this opportune time, to begin dealing in Hungarian wines with your husband's father, while he is yet alive? Your husband might join his father and so learn thoroughly all the details of the Hungarian wine trade, which, if conducted by people who understand it, brings in a handsome profit". She also spoke similarly to me; and, beeing deeply moved by my father's grief, I made up my mind to proceed with him to Hungary and to purchase wine. I took along with me all my available cash, a sum of 80 ducats. We made our way through the town of Drohobycz, where we had to exchange our Polish money for the Hungarian *maryash*,[1] the imperial coins current in Hungary. Wherever my father went, his own cleverness and the assistance of his friends — at Drohobycz the well-known R. Salman, son of Bine, and at Turka[2] the landlord of the township, Kalinowski[3] — enabled him to change all my money without the slightest loss. In those days merchants travelling to Hungary had to buy imperial currency at a great loss.

My father was welcomed everywhere; people were glad to see him again, Jews and Gentiles alike. Above all they were pleased with his charming manner of speech to everybody, Jews and Gentiles, both in Poland and in Hungary. They liked to listen to his tales and proverbs in Yiddish, Polish and Hungarian, for he had perfectly mastered these languages. My father once acted as interpreter between Rakoczy, the King of Hungary, and Sieniawski,

[1] Old 20 kreuzer pieces.
[2] Situated in the Carpathian Mountains in Galicia.
[3] John Kalinowski, Vice-Chamberlain of Pernau.

the Commander-in-Chief of the Polish Army, as related on page...[1]

My father traversed Hungary with me, and in every single place where wines were to be found he explained to me the qualities and quantities of the local vintages. This knowledge he imparted even when no purchases were made, with the purpose of familiarising me with the kinds of wine to be obtained in the various markets. Most of all I learned from his accounts of the experience he had gathered in dealing in wine and in other kinds of business which he had carried on all his life. He recounted how the Lord in His great mercy and compassion had always protected him, how he had been saved from fearful dangers, as related before on page... and how he had been saved from death.[2]

We arrived at the town of Miskolcz, where my brother, Aryeh Loeb, was purchasing wine; he was staying with the *Kazin* R. Abraham Schpilke, a wholesale merchant, and at that time the foremost of all the Jewish residents of Miskolcz. My brother bought all the wine he needed from Count Gvadanyi,[3] a former officer in the Emperor's army, who in his old age lived at Miskolcz. Being very rich, Gvadanyi carried on a great business in various kinds of goods, and especially in wine, which he purchased from the inhabitants of that town, and sold at a profit. From his stock my brother obtained all the wine that he wanted, of the best qualities, produced from selected fine

---

[1] Francis II (Rakoczy) spent some time (1702—1703) in disguise as a civil engineer on the estates of Adam Nicholas Sieniawski, the Voyevoda of Belz and Grand Hetman of the Polish Army. The exiled King thus gained the support of the Hetman and his wife, a lady who was much interested in political affairs. After his defeat in the battle of Trenczin, in 1710 (see Hengelmueller, *Hungary's Fight for National Existence*, 1913), Rakoczy escaped to Poland, making his way through the Carpathian Mountains. The page referred to by Ber has not been preserved, so that we do not know on what occasion his father acted as interpreter between the Hungarian King and the Polish Hetman.

[2] These stories are not preserved in the Memoirs.

[3] A renowned Hungarian county family in the county of Borsod.

máslás of the year 1742.[1] The price agreed to between my
brother and the Count was 8 ducats per cask of that
wine, and the same sum per barrel (or *antal*) of wine
made from dried grapes.

My father had heard of my brother's dealings before
our arrival at Miskolcz, while we were still on our way
to the place. When we arrived there he did not go to
the inn in which my brother stayed, but we rode through
another street and took lodging in the house of an Hungarian silversmith. The silversmith was no longer alive;
his aged widow gave my father a special room, and as-
signed the horses a stable near a small stream, where they
could be well watered. Near this house lived R. Isaac
Kretser, whose wife, a native of Skole, came of a good
family, with which my father was friendly. My father
gave this lady money to buy so many pounds of meat,
and he himself bought fine large fish; and she consented
to prepare suitable dishes for us, and did so as long as
we stayed there.

One day a cooper recognized my father and said to
him: "A Hungarian noble has come to his house here in
Miskolcz from a long way off, from his estates in Upper
Hungary, fourty leages from here. He has fine grounds,
vineyards and buildings, and vaults full of excellent wines.
He has not been here for three years, and during all that
time not one cask of wine has been sold. When he gets
to know you as a merchant in a good way of business, he
will certainly sell you good wine at a reasonable price."
So we went with the cooper to the noble, who was pleased
to meet my father, and sent one of his men to show us
all his wines. My father chose what we needed — several
casks of good *máslás*, and also some barrels of wine made
from dried grapes, which is called in Polish *suchyjagod*,
of the famous vintage of 502 (1742). My father agreed to
pay 4 ducats for each cask of *máslás*, and the same for

---

[1] This is one of the very rare occasions on which the author quotes the
year of the common era.

each barrel of *suchyjagod*. We took as much of the wine as we needed, and were able to pay in cash.

We had to stay in this town ten days, until the carts arrived to carry the wines to Munkacs.[1] The noble was good enough to order a large bundle of hay to be given each day to our horses, and two bottles of good wine for my father's use, besides a loaf of fine wheat bread to the carter, who was deputed by the owners of the carts to wait upon us until the arrival of the carts, in accordance with the usual custom. The noble's servants gave this carter daily a loaf of wheat bread, and a piece of fat bacon. The wine which was given to us every day made a whole barrel of good *máslás*, and some of it we found useful for filling up other barrels.

When this transaction was finished I visited my brother in the inn of R. Abraham Schpilke. I saw on the window-sills some samples of wines, and my brother gave me some to taste; the taste both of the *máslás* and of the *suchyjagod* was just like that of the wines which my father had just bought, as they had been grown in the same year, and mixed and prepared in the same way. My brother told me the price of them: every cask and every barrel had cost him 8 ducats. I went at once and brought my brother our samples; I let him taste them, and he recognised that they were of one and the same quality. My brother then admitted that my father was of all Jewish merchants the greatest connoisseur in the wine business, and the most experienced in the details of the trade.

After leaving Miskolcz we reached the village of Luk, on the banks of the great river Theiss, with all our wines. Here Wolf Kamrash, the lessee of the "tolerance tax",[2]

---

[1] Town in Upper Hungary, in the district of Carpatho-Ruthenia. now belonging to Czecho-Slovakia.

[2] This tax was introduced in Hungary by Queen Maria Theresa in 1743 and 1749. The Hungarian Jews paid it until 1846. See B. Bernstein, *Die Toleranztaxe der Juden in Ungarn*, in *Gedenkbuch zur Erinnerung an David Kaufmann*, 1900, pp. 599—628. This Wolf Kamrash was, according to Ber, one of the collectors of the tax.

tried to do us a mischief. He found a lot of soldiers of
the imperial army in the village, showed them documents
proving that he was the holder of the "tolerance tax",
and told them that as the revenues of this tax were due
to the Empress' treasury, all soldiers of the imperial army
were bound to help him and do his bidding when he
needed them. He also plied them with brandy and beer
until they were drunk. When my father arrived at Luk
he at once saw through the trick. Neither R. Wolf nor
the soldiers had any right to stop waggons loaded with
goods on the highway, for merchants had to pay duties
to the crown only in towns situated on the frontiers. The
soldiers, hearing this from my father, withdrew and paid
no more attention to R. Wolf, but said: "It is not for us
to interfere in the affairs of merchants and to stop them
with their goods." So the waggons passed over the river,
and we reached our home in Bolechow with our wines.
My brother brought his wines to Lemberg, his partner,
the noble, having obtained permission from the Franciscan
friars to store the wines in the vaults of the cloister, whence
my brother sold them all. We sold our little stock to
the nobles of our neighbourhood.

At that time R. Elieser Ashkenasi came for the first
time from Nagy-Karoly to purchase horses for the Hungarian army, for which purpose he was provided with
large sums from the imperial treasury. He stayed at Stryi
in the house of R. Zebi Hirsch, son of Mordechai. About
the same time R. Simon Masatner, his brother-in-law, passed
through Bolechow. Seeing my horse, on which I had ridden
from the Fair at Dolina, he wanted to buy it, and I sold it
to him for ten ducats, having paid for it only three days before five ducats and twelve Polish gulden. He asked me to
get him some more horses, and I procured him three more
fine animals, which he and his brother-in-law purchased.
I made with the help of Providence over 3oo gulden, which
in my young days was considered a very good profit.

At that time there was in our community a certain
R. Tobias, son of R. Reuben, who was a very honest

man, and an old friend of my brother Bendet. Seeing that I showed aptitude for business, and having heard that there had been brought to Tysmienica a large quantity of ewes' wool, suitable for making crimson girdles, he asked my brother to suggest to me that I should go to Tysmienica to buy the wool. "As your brother", he said, "does not understand which kinds of wool are good and which are bad, I will send with him on horseback, at my own expense, a man who thoroughly understands wool, and knows what each kind is good for." So he sent with me R. Ber, son of R. Judah, a merchant who was an expert in wool. We went to Tysmienica, where we negotiated with the Armenian [1] Girek Karila and his sons, who had brought four large waggons [2] full of choice wool fit for spinning.

.....[3] and he was dismissed from his post. My brother pleaded before the Princess [4] on behalf of our community of Bolechow, putting the case of our brethren eloquently before her. She was persuaded by him, and ordered the transfer of the revenues of the *Gabelle* [5] to the treasury of the community.

But — for our great sins — while my brother was at Warsaw, occupied with the aforesaid affairs, and I was at Lemberg, busy with the sale of our stock of wine, I dreamed a bad dream — that my wife had severe labour

[1] Tysmienica was famous by reason of its Armenian traders, who enjoyed special privileges granted to them by the owners of the town. See S. Barącz, *Pamiętnik dziejów Polskich*, 1855.

[2] The text has *Karawusz*. According to Linde, *Dictionary of the Polish language*, this word is derived from the Wallachian *Kereuszie*, and means "a loaded waggon". The *Encyklopedya Powszechna*, 1863, v. XIV. p. 71, rejects Linde's conjecture, and says that *Karawusz* (from Turkish *Karawesz*) means "slave" or "servant". Ber's use of *Karawusz* seems, however, to confirm Linde's interpretation.

[3] The beginning of this fragment of the Manuscript is not preserved.

[4] Princess Lubomirska.

[5] Tax from ritual slaughter. See Introduction p. 36.

with child; and on the following morning sad news reached
me from our community. On Sunday, the 13th of Tammuz,
519 (8th July 1759) there came 28 Russians (Ruthenians)
from the mountains, ruffians called *Opryszki* (footpads).[1]
It was at dawn, after the night watch had gone off to their
houses for their morning sleep. The band stopped before
the house of the *Każin*, R. Nahman, and there found the fire
made by the guard still burning. Near the fire the beadle
of the community, R. Hirsch *Schulklopper*, was sleeping,
having under his head the big kettledrum of the town.
R. Hirsch awoke, and the bandits threw the drum into
the fire, where it was burnt. Then they ordered the beadle
to call to the people in the house to open the door for
him, so that they might not suspect the presence of the
bandits. Hirschel[2] did so, and when the door was opened
the robbers rushed into the rooms, where they found
the son-in-law of R. Naḥman, R. Abraham, the Rabbi of
Dolina. R. Naḥman had already fled to another room,
which had a strong vaulted ceiling, and with him his
wife and daughter (Abraham's wife), together with a woman attendant. Thus only Naḥman's son-in-law fell into
the hands of the bandits. He begged for mercy, and tried
to escape by saying: "I am only tutor to the children in the
house of this wealthy man, and he will not give a farthing
for my ransom; even if you kill me he will not care."

Meanwhile the learned *Każin*, R. Ber, son of Aryeh Loeb,
awoke from his sleep, hearing that the robbers were in

---

[1] The bands of ruffians called *opryszki*, armed with rifles and axes, were
in those days the terror of the population in the district situated north of
the Carpathians, and particularly of merchants going to and coming from
Hungary. These bandits, Ruthenians (Ukrainians) by nationality, lived in the
mountains, where they used to attack travellers in the defiles and make raids
upon the towns and villages. The very name *Opryszki* made the population
so frightened that no resistance was offered to the bandits even if they
appeared in small numbers. In spite of the severe measures taken by the
authorities, the activities of the bands continued for many years. — See
S. Barącz, *Pamiątki miasta Stanisławowa*, (1858), p. 88, and K. Rakowski,
Wewnętrzne dzieje Polski (1908), p. 401.

[2] Diminutive of Hirsch.

the town, and rushed out of his house in alarm, undressed except for his night-shirt. He tried to escape through the back gate of his house, hoping that the robbers would not notice him. But some of the robbers, who were keeping watch at the back gate of Naḥman's house, saw Ber running away, and caught hold of him by his shirt and brought him to their companions. He begged for mercy, promising to pay a handsome ransom for his life, and led the bandits to the vaulted chamber in the house of Naḥ-man, where his mother Reisel slept. (This lady carried on a retail business in various articles on these premises, after the death of her husband Aryeh Loeb, son of Isaac.) The martyr[1] R. Ber cried out: "Mother! Mother! Open the door, and give the ransom for my life;" but his mother was afraid to open the door.

The Rabbi of Dolina, R. Abraham, was still in the hands of the robbers, and R. Ber told them that he was R. Naḥman's son-in-law, but R. Abraham said: "I am only tutor to R. Naḥman's sons, but this gentleman is his son." Thus the robbers, who had just heard R. Ber calling "Mother! Mother!", believed that he must be R. Naḥman's son.

R. Naḥman himself, however, as I have said, had taken refuge with his wife, his daughter and a woman attendant in the vaulted room, the doors of which were of iron and were locked and barred with iron bars. The robbers tried to force these iron doors. R. Naḥman then took his firearm and shot one of the band dead. This made the others furious, and they started to break down the iron shutters with large pieces of stout wood and to get in by the windows. R. Naḥman then said: "I will give you money in silver coins," and threw a sack full of silver coins through the iron bars of the window, containing, as he said, 3000 gulden; and the sack burst open and the coins rolled through the cellar windows into the cellar. R. Naḥman

---

[1] The author, in anticipation of the tragic end of R. Ber, calls him a martyr.

had to fire on them twice more with the two firearms he had in his hands, full of powder and shot. With one shot he wounded one of the robbers in the foot, and with the other he wounded the chief of the band, Ivan Boytchuk, below the chest, but not mortally. When the chief felt the pain of the wound, he commanded his fellows in Ruthenian: "*Molodtzy, palitj*", that is to say, "My lads, burn the house over his head!" The street-sellers who stood in front of R. Naḥman's house by day used to leave the boxes containing their wares in his house overnight for safe keeping. The robbers seized these boxes, threw away their contents, chopped up the boxes with their axes, and with the wood set fire to all four corners of the building, so, that it might burn quickly.

The bandits then vented their anger upon the martyr R. Ber, who was still in their hands, together with R. Abraham. They believed R. Abraham's statement that R. Ber was a son of R. Naḥman, beause they had heard him crying to his mother to open the door; and consequently, for our great sins, they beat him to death with their axes. A woman named Etti, daughter of Malkah, who was then the midwife, came and implored the bandits to spare R. Ber; and one of them struck her down with his axe, and she died on the spot on which R. Ber had fallen, in front of R. Naḥman's house. They also murdered a certain Eisik, son of the shopkeeper R. Loeb, who came to plead with them to spare his little shop; and the bodies of both Etti and Eisik were burnt, and not a trace of them could be found. But R. Ber, although struck to earth, felt the heat of the fire, and had sufficient strength to drag himself away from the spot to the main street, where he expired, giving up his soul in holiness and purity. The people brought R. Ber's corpse to the synagogue and laid it on the large table placed at the entrance. This table now stands on the southern side of the *Beth-ha-Midrash*; for more than thirty years the marks of the blood which had run from this martyr could be seen on it.

This R. Ber was once on his way to Breslau, at a time when Prince Martin Lubomirski[1] had set out on a plundering expedition, and had robbed many merchants and murdered not a few. R. Ber would have fallen into his hands, had it not been that a wheel of the cart was broken, and this accident delayed him a night. In the meantime the Prince with his retinue went away, and R. Ber was saved. He returned home in safety on a Friday, the 11th of *Tammuz*, and on the Sabbath he was called to the *Torah* and recited the thanksgiving prayer for having been rescued. Because of our great sins he did not know that he was destined to die in his own house, which seemed to be a safe place. Though he had plenty of money with which to ransom himself, he could not annul the decree (of heaven), and he died at the early age of thirty-six. He was a man of learning, strong and wealthy, tall, well-built and handsome. He left not his like in our community, and since his death there has been none like him.

The Rabbi of Dolina was still held by the bandits, who spared him on his promising to show them the houses of other rich Jews besides R. Naḥman. He guided them to the houses of R. Judah (son of R. Aaron) and of his son R. Eisik, but both had escaped with their families when they learned that the robbers had come to the town. The robbers, finding an empty house, started to loot it, and while they were thus engaged R. Abraham escaped to the other side of the river and joined the other Jews who had fled thither.

At the same time two of the band broke into the house of my brother, R. Aryeh Loeb, and found in the front room his wife Rachel, who had just jumped out of her bed and was not dressed. They mistook her for a maid, and wounded her in the head with an axe. They then rushed into the inner part of the house, and she took refuge in the oven, but with great difficulty, for she was

---

[1] Apparently the general, Martin Lubomirski, notorious for his adventurous life. See A. Boniecki and A. Rejski, *Polish Heraldry* (P.), 1912, vol. XV.

tall and stout. Learning later that a fire had broken
out in the town, she left the oven in great alarm, not
noticing that her earrings, set with valuable and beautiful diamonds, had fallen from her ears. However, she
not only escaped from the fire, but saved all her jewels
and costly dresses, for she was a clever and energetic
woman.

In the meanwhile two other robbers had entered my
house and found my wife Leah still in bed. They demanded
a large sum of money, whereupon my wife gave them a
ducat and 20 gulden, apologising that she had not another
farthing in ready money. One of them hit her cruel blows
with an axe on her arm and back, so that the flesh and
skin remained black for a long time. They commanded
her to hand over to them the golden ornaments and pearls.
Some said that the Gentile inhabitants of our town had
informed the robbers that they would find such things in my
house. My wife had to hand over all her precious things:
two necklaces of fine and beautiful pearls, one of four rows
and the other of five rows, a head-dress of great value
and beauty, and ten gold rings set with magnificent and
rare diamonds. The value of all these things amounted
at that time to 3ooo gulden. Besides this the robbers took
away the furniture, and burnt the house, which was valued
then at 4ooo gulden. My total loss thus amounted to 7ooo
gulden. Just then the bandits heard that the fire was
spreading, and they left my wife, who escaped to the
other side of the river. The maid, a Muscovite woman,
remained behind, and saved everything she could carry
from the fire, including my books, about hundred in number,
most of them by ancient authors. She took pity on the
books because she knew that I was fond of them, and
therefore thought she must save them. She carried them
off in a sack, in two journeys, and did not leave a single
one behind. But twelve good books were missing from my
collection, for they had been stolen by my neighbours.
Nine years later I recognised two of those books, and
they were returned to me.

On Monday, the 14th of *Tammuz* (9th July), this sad
news reached me. I hired a cart and left Lemberg. After
a whole night's travel I met one of our community, who
had been sent to Lemberg to tell me what had happened
at Bolechow. I arrived there on Tuesday evening, the
15th of *Tammuz*, 519 (10th July, 1759). The whole town
was in a great uproar, and the people greatly troubled
and distressed.[1] The band had left the town triumphantly
a little before midnight on the Sunday. When they entered
the town some members of our community had run to the
church and tolled the bell, to call the people to help;
and when the bandits heard the bells ringing, one of them
shot R. Bezalel, son of R. Loeb, in his leg, and he remained
lame to the time of his death. A Gentile who was standing
near the bells was also wounded by a shot. Consequently
nobody attempted to stop the bandits, who went about
in safety and worked their will. The bandit who had been
wounded in his leg by R. Naḥman was placed on a horse
which they took from some Gentiles who had come to
to attend the Fair of St. Peter; and the rest took sixteen
horses from riders whom they met, and rode away on
them. They dressed themselves in silk ladies' dresses
which they had stolen in the town — skirts of damask
and satin and other materials of red, green, blue and other
colours. The chief of the band put on himself the white
Leibserdak[2] of my brother R. Aryeh Loeb, which he had
had made for the Passover. It was of white lustrine of
the finest quality, with beautiful silver tassels, and covered
with good *sitrakas*.[3] The bandits also made a flag from
an apron of brocade of very fine silk, embroidered with
gold and silver, which they put on a stick, and this flag
they carried in front of their chief.

So the band departed in safety, and no one pursued
them, for the steward who was then in command of the

---

[1] According to Ber's note in his work *Dibré Binah*, nine people were
killed by the bandits. See *Hashiloaḥ*, vol. 38, p. 445.

[2] The traditional garment with fringes on the borders.

[3] I have been unable to discover the meaning of this word.

fortress at Bolechow was not at home, having spent the
night at Stryi. Everybody was angry at his absence from
the town during the pillage and fire, for they thought
that if he could not have prevented the bandits from looting, he might at least have saved something from the fire,
as the Gentiles would have felt obliged to put out the fire
and to save some of the buildings, had the steward commanded them to do so.

This steward was a good friend of mine, and liked me
very much. He had spent one Saturday with me at the
township of Lisko, during the last Passover, as I have
related on page . . , having been sent with me by the
priest Wieniawski, the Dean of Lemberg, to buy Hungarian wines. Being young and inexperienced, he had to
follow my advice in keeping the account books in proper
order. After this Wieniawski appointed him to be the
steward of our town. He remained a true friend to me
all his life, even after he left Bolechow and was made
steward of the town of Komarno; and whenever he came
to Lemberg he visited me and enquired after my welfare
with great affection.

Then, after the robbery and the great fire, the steward
and I had a conference with a number of noblemen,
persons of intelligence and judgment, and they all came
to an agreement as to the best way of helping the ruined
town. First of all an enquiry into the amount of each
person's loss was to be made by trustworthy noblemen,
who were acquainted with the people of our town and
knew the value of everyone's house and everyone's business and affairs — the shopkeepers, the innkeepers and
the other big and small traders. These noblemen estimated
the value of the buildings and goods destroyed by fire.
The whole work fell on the leaders of the community,
who were at that time the learned R. Isaac, of Brody,
R. Ber Kaz, son of R. Naḥman, the learned R. Isaac Eisik,
son of R. Judah, and myself, Ber, son of R. Judah. The
three first mentioned did not understand what benefit would
result from this investigation. I, therefore, had to insist on

the steward's persisting in this enquiry with all his energy. With that end in view he invited many noblemen from the neighbourhood, including the aged Madarake, Hoszowski, Ilnicki, and also the judge of the town and the members of the Municipal Council of Bolechow. They all went with us to view the sites of the demolished buildings, in order to determine the value of the premises before they had fallen victims to the flames, and the amount and value of the goods that were stored in them. All these particulars were tabulated in proper order in a register of sixteen sheets. The amount of the damage caused by the fire to the Jews of our town was calculated at 300,000 gulden.

The register was written out in triplicate and signed by the nobles, who acted as witnesses, and the members of the Municipal Council. One copy was sent to Lemberg to the headquarters of the administration of the excise of beer, mead and spirituous liquors distilled from corn,[1] which used to collect from Bolechow every year taxes amounting to more than 500 gulden. When the documents reached the officials of the administration at Lemberg, they took pity on the people of our town, who had suffered by fire and looting, and excused them from paying this tax for a period of five years, during which we did not pay a farthing.

The second copy of the register was sent to Brody, to the Elders of the Central and Provincial (Jewish) Assemblies in Poland,[2] by the hand of R. Aryeh Loeb, son of R. Kalman Kaz. We also gave him letters, skilfully written in the proper style of the holy language, telling the story of the ruin of our community and of the great losses of its members through the robbery and the fire. The reply was: "An abatement will be allowed to your community." But some of the Elders ironically remarked:

[1] This excise, in Polish *Czopowe i szelążne*, was introduced in 1629 and was fixed at the tenth *grosz* of the net proceeds of the spirit trade. See Introduction, p. 37.

[2] These institutions are described in the Introduction to the present book, p. 38—39.

"With so poor a letter it is fitting to sit at the entrance to a cemetery and to ask for alms!" So R. Aryeh Loeb, son of R. Kalman Kaz, returned to our community without a proper answer.

The third copy of the register was sent by the Elders of our community to the town of Rzeszow, through R. Abraham Charmat, the son-in-law of R. Michel Tranes. He set out on a horse and appeared before the Princess,[1] the ruler of our town, with a supplication, that is, a great petition craving pity for our community after the pillage and fire from which the people of Bolechow had suffered. The Princess was touched by the fate of our people, and wrote a letter to the State Treasurer of the Crown, asking him to show us favour and pleading strongly on our behalf. R. Abraham rode to the town of Pilica and there handed the letter to the State Treasurer, Wessel,[2] who sent the following reply to the Princess: "What can I do now? The taxing authorities have completed the assessment of the taxes, and the assignations[3] have been distributed in the name of all the Jewish Elders, who assembled in a great congress at great expense. It is quite impossible to call another congress. All that the community of Bolechow can do is to ask the people of the neighbouring communities, who know it, to contribute more than their due in taxes to the Crown, and thus to give relief to the community which has suffered by fire."

The following reply was accordingly sent from Rzeszow in the name of the Princess by one of her stewards, Tinecki, to the Elders of our community: "At present there is, according to the letter of the State Treasurer to the Prin-

---

[1] Princess Johanna Lubomirska.

[2] Theodor Wessel was appointed State Treasurer in August 1761. The fire occured in July, 1759, and the various petitions of Ber and his fellow-citizens must have been sent in soon afterwards. At that time the State Treasurer of Poland was Charles Siedlnicki. Our author wrote in his old age, and apparently overlooked this fact. — Pilica, a town in the district of Radom, was the property of the family of Wessel.

[3] In Polish administrative law, an instruction given to pay out money.

cess, no way of obtaining relief except to approach your neighbouring communities and request them to take an additional burden on their shoulders in order to relieve you. This is because you did not hasten to send your representative during the session of the Elders of the Council of Four Lands,[1] and when you did do so you sent a person as illiterate as a calf, who did not know how to answer the Treasurer and how to apologize for the delay in submitting your request to him."

The people of our community were greatly distressed and dismayed, being afraid of the hard measures which might be taken by the soldiers of the Polish army, who used to come in their carts and on horses to all the Jewish communities to collect the tax for the Crown, that is, the poll-tax. As the Jews always held that it was forbidden to number the people, because of what happened in the days of King David, who was punished (for having numbered his people), but repented and confessed (his sin),[2] special arrangements were made in the Capital, Warsaw, during the sessions of the Diet between the Crown and the Members of the Senate on the one hand, and the Chiefs and Leaders of the Jewish Central and Provincial Assemblies of Poland on the other hand. The Jewish Elders pledged themselves to estimate and to appraise what every community was able to pay every year in taxes, and the Polish troops were then ordered to collect the taxes from each community, as I have related above.

But God, the Mighty, does not reject the seed of Israel, and does not forsake his people. During the time of the fairs, which I spent at Lemberg, a noble of my acquaintance visited me and told me that he was a bearer of good news. "I have received", he said, "an assignation from the State Treasurer on the poll-tax due from the community of Bolechow to the amount of 2100 gulden. I shall be in your town, and will see your wife, who is

[1] See Introduction, p. 36.
[2] II Sam. 23.

as respected as her husband." So he talked in the usual
hypocritical manner of the nobles, but I was very angry.
Some salt-merchants also happened to be staying at
Lemberg, and I sent for them. R. Wolf and the learned
Kazin, R. Israel, son of R. Naḥman, came to me, and
when they heard the news they realized what a blunder
the heads of our community had made in sending R. Abraham Charmat as our representative to Rzeszow and afterwards to Pilica to see the State Treasurer, as I have
related above.

The noble told them also that he had an assignation
on the community of Bolechow to the amount of 2100 gulden in accordance with the estimate made by the taxing
authorities [1] elected by the Heads of the Jewish Assembly.
R. Wolf and R. Israel began to plead with the noble, and
told him of the great devastation caused by the pillage
and the fire. They further said that there were no Chiefs
of the community, nor beadles either, because some of
them had been killed by the bandits, and no others had
yet been appointed in their place. The people of Bolechow were thus left without a leader. Very few of the
inhabitants remained there, the majority having removed
from Bolechow and gone to establish themselves in other
communities where they could find a living. The noble
was moved by the story of the great ruin which had
fallen upon the town of Bolechow, and said: "There is
no other way for you but to approach the paymaster
of our troops, that is, the Army Secretary of the Crown, [2]
in whose hands the assignation now is; he is the landlord of the town of Rozdol. [3] Tell him about the great
ruin of your town, and perhaps he may be willing to
assist you."

---

[1] Special officials of the staff of the Jewish Assemblies.

[2] Wenceslaus Rzewuski, Army Secretary of the Crown. — B. Connor,
A History of Poland, (p. 16) calls these officers the "Camp Notaries", who
were the paymasters-general for the Army both of the Kingdom (Poland)
and of the Duchy (Lithuania).

[3] Town in Galicia.

R. Joseph[1] and R. Israel agreed to go to this officer on condition that I accompanied them, and we went to him and explained the ruin of our town. Rzewuski[2] replied: "I will wait for your payment until the next festival of St. John."[3] Then he looked at me and asked: "Does this merchant also live in Bolechow?" R. Israel, son of R. Naḥman, said: "He is a dealer in Hungarian wine, a native of Bolechow, and he always sells his wine at Lemberg." Rzewuski then said: "I will wait until the festival of St John, but if you do not pay in time this merchant's wine will also belong to me." I was very indignant at what R. Israel had said, and asked why he had spoken so to this noble, who, as was notorious, daily robbed without mercy the community of Rozdol and the communities in his other towns, imposing heavy payments upon them, and instigating people to accuse them wrongfully in order that they might buy off the libellers by paying money.[4] I lifted my eyes to Heaven and said: "Thence will come my help; the Lord deliver me from evil happenings." The matter remained in suspense until the time for the payment at the festival of St. John.

After the Passover in 520 (1760) I returned from my home to Lemberg in order to sell the wines which I had there. My brother, Aryeh Loeb, had commenced to rebuild his house, and during the winter all the timber for the building had been got ready. As both my brother's house and mine were burned down, we had to go and live with our father, after having repaired at our expense a large part of the roof of his house, which had been damaged by the flames. We both went to stay with our father at the festival of the New Year of 520 (22d September 1759), and my brother

---

[1] Called above R. Wolf.

[2] See footnote 2 on page 106.

[3] 24th June, 1760.

[4] See article "Rozdol", in the *Jewish Encyclopedia*, (in Russian), vol. XIII, in which mention is made of the lawsuits which lasted for years between Rzewuski and the Jews on account of the increased taxes which Rzewuski had imposed on the Jewish inhabitants of his estates.

invited our father to the New Year's feast. He sat at the
first table by our father's side, and his wife Rachel sat
with them; I sat with my wife and my son at the second
table. During the meal on the first day of the feast my
father rose from his seat and came to sit near me to share
our company, where he finished his meal; and after that
he never sat at my brother's table during the whole winter.
Although living with all of us, he never tasted any of the
cooking of Rachel, my brother's wife, but shared my meals
until his death. My brother, therefore, felt compelled to
hasten the building of his house, as he saw that my father
did not care for his staying with him. He asked his wife
to treat our venerable father, who was then 87 years old,
with the regard due to a man of his age and position. The
remainder of my dealings with my father, in connection
with the sale of his house to me, I will soon relate in
their proper place.

Now I have to return to my subject. I was forced
to leave my wife and my son with my father whilst
my brother, Aryeh Loeb, remained at Bolechow super-
vising the building of his home, and I went alone to
Lemberg to sell the remainder of our wines. Walking
into the town after the Passover I met R. Joseph, son of
R. Seinwel, from our community, who had brought cartloads of salt to sell. It happened that the nobleman who
held the assignation on the poll-tax, which amounted to
2100 gulden, came upon us. He recognised us and said:
"What do you intend to do? The festival of St. John
is approaching, and I shall have to come to your town
with my horsemen, armed, to collect the taxes." I at once
replied: "I do not worry about that, as I do not belong
to Bolechow any longer." I had in fact settled at Lemberg at the request of the Heads of both Jewish communities at Lemberg, as I will relate in due course.[1] The nobleman said: "If so, I will go to my friend's house and make
the acquaintance of his respected wife." So he went with

---

[1] Not preserved in the MS.

us. I promptly sent my assistant Israel, of Tolcsva,[1] (now an important person in Hungary; he was an intelligent and clever youth) to Khule, the wife of R. Abele, son of R. Schabsel from Stryi, a neighbour of mine, to ask her in my name to come to my house and to receive the nobleman and entertain him in the Polish language, after the fashion of gentle people, and to make him believe that she was my wife. She came to my house, received him as hostess, and ordered a bottle of good wine, which he drank; and he believed her to be my wife. I was forced to do all this, because I was frightened by the threat of Rzewuski (the owner of Rozdol) who, when he learned from R. Israel, son of R. Naḥman, that I was dealing in Hungarian wines in Lemberg, said that he would seize my wines if the poll-taxes for the Crown were not paid in time. Meanwhile R. Joseph started to talk and to describe to the noble the great devastation caused in Bolechow by the robbers and the fire. I reinforced his tale, with more and more exaggeration. I said: "Although I have left that place, my heart is heavy for my relatives and friends there, who are cast out in hunger and in privation. They that were brought up in scarlet embrace dunghills.[2] They have no houses, their own having perished in the flames; they are thrown into the street, and are truly deserving of pity. Nobody ought to demand from them even a farthing. I would offer my lord a gift of 10 ducats if he would plead for the people of Bolechow and save them from the payment of that debt." He listened in silence to our pleading, and without saying another word went his way.

Some days later there arrived at Lemberg, on his way from Hungary to Muscovy, a German, the master of the mint at Kremnitz,[3] where the noted gold coins are stamped. He was a Gentile, a well-to-do person and a very clever

---

[1] Township in Hungary, in the county of Zemplén, now belonging to Czecho-Slovakia.

[2] Lam. 4[5].

[3] Or Körmöczbanya.

man. But as he did not know a word of Polish, he was compelled to seek a lodging in my house, so that he could
be understood, and I gave him a room to himself. The
next day he asked me to take him to the town, as he
wanted to buy some summer articles. On our way home
a carriage passed in which was the nobleman who was
to receive the amount of the poll-tax. He called me to
him, and said: "Follow me to my house, I have to speak
with you." I was terribly frightened, as I thought that
he was going to arrest me for the taxes, which our community was to pay, but trusting in God I followed the
carriage. The nobleman got out of the carriage, gave
his arm to his lady to escort her to her apartments, and
said to me: "Wait here, I will come to you at once."
I then understood that there was no reason to fear, as
he did not call me into the house. He soon came back,
and said: "The matter is settled now", and he drew out
a letter from the noble Rzewuski and read it to me. Its
purport was that he had ordered that the community of
Bolechow should not be pressed for payment till the
next Assembly of the Council of Four Lands, which was
expected to meet soon. The noble continued: "I shall
have to go to Bolechow to ascertain whether your statements are right. If they are, you will surely be freed
from payment of the taxes. You should write quickly to
the Heads of your community to give me the 12 ducats
which I was promised.[1] I will certainly do all I can to
advocate your cause and to save you from this payment."
I went at once and wrote to my brother, R. Aryeh Loeb,
and to the community, advising them to do their best to
secure the favour of this nobleman. I was very annoyed
about his going there, because our people had in the
meantime built many houses finer than before. I tried to
persuade him not to go, on the ground that no chief or
beadle had been appointed that year in the community,
and that there was no proper house for his accommodation

[1] Previously only 10 ducats were mentioned.

there. But he said: "I must go, having been told to do so by
the pay-officer Rzewuski, but I will do what I can for you."

The noble went on his way and met in Stryi my brother,
Aryeh Loeb. They had a long talk, and went to the wine-
shop of R. Hirsch, son of R. Mordechai, who dealt in
Hungarian wine. My brother ordered some good wine for
the nobleman, who took note of what my brother said to
him, and they agreed that he should not go to Bolechow;
he went back to Lemberg and handed me a letter from
my brother, on which I had to pay him the 12 ducats.

After his arrival there he demanded from me the 12 ducats in accordance with the letter. I discussed with the
noble how I should receive the money later on, and we
agreed that he should give me a document saying that
after the community of Bolechow had paid the amount
of the taxes — 2100 gulden —, as estimated,[1] 10 ducats
would be put down to the account of the community, and
2 ducats be allowed me for my trouble in advocating the
cause of the community of Bolechow. All the time he
believed that I had moved my home to Lemberg. He
accordingly reported to his master, the pay-officer Rzewuski, on the great ruin which had overtaken that town
and the poverty of its inhabitants, from whom it appeared
impossible to extract any money, whereupon the latter
returned the assignation to the State Treasurer, who paid
Rzewuski in cash the amount of that assignation, i. e.
2100 gulden.

During the following session of the Assembly of the
Council of Four Lands, the Elders had to return to the
State Treasurer this sum, which put them to great expense. But this affair was of advantage to our community
as regards payment of taxes for the future, as I shall
relate further in its place.

Now we return to the affairs of our wine business.
In 520 (1760) I went with my brother, R. Aryeh Loeb,

[1] The whole matter was, it should be remembered, delayed till the next
session of the Council of Four Lands.

to Hungary to buy some wine. We stopped at Talya,[1]
where we made a purchase of 28 casks of good *máslás*
wine at the price of 280 ducats, that is, 10 ducats per cask.
Moreover, we acquired 15 barrels of wine made from dry
grapes, each barrel at the price of 8 ducats. At another
place, Tarczal, we bought from the cellars of the Crown
100 casks of ordinary quality. We managed to sell all
these wines, but the *máslás* had to be stored for a certain
time. It was, therefore, necessary to collect enough money
to buy new wines for the needs of our business.

There was, however, another reason for the decrease of
our capital. The Elders of the Four Lands realized that the
payment of the taxes for the community of Bolechow out
of their own pocket would be a great burden for them, and
therefore, decided to compromise with the people of our
town. At their session held in Brody[2] they wrote a letter
to the Elders of the community at Bolechow, asking them
to send representatives with whom they could settle the
question of the taxes. The Fair of St. George[3] was just
approaching, and some of our people at Bolechow were
preparing to visit it, viz., R. Simel and R. Isaac, son-
in-law of R. Nathan. These two members of our community were accordingly appointed to talk over the matter
of the taxes with the Elders of the Four Lands, and were
given a letter to this end, written and sealed by the
Elders of our community. Both R. Simel and R. Isaac
went to Brody. There they handed the letter to the
Elders of the Four Lands, and entered into a discussion
over the taxes to be paid, but they could not give any
satisfactory explanation, and were thus unable to settle

[1] County of Zemplen, district of Szerencs.

[2] This session took place apparently in 1761.

[3] According to Barącz, *The Free Commercial Town of Brody* (P.),
p. 93 and 96, Fairs were held in Brody on the Day of St. George of the
Greek Church, which fell on the 23rd April of the Julian Calendar, which
corresponded in the eighteenth century to the 5th May of the Gregorian
Calendar. Dr. Lewin's combinations in his *Neue Materialien etc.*, 1916, p. 9,
are, therefore, futile.

the matter. The Elders sitting at Brody then addressed another letter to the community at Bolechow, which ran: "If you desire to come to an understanding with us, send us reliable men." Thereupon the people at Bolechow asked my brother, Aryeh Loeb, to go there himself and to bring about an agreement. My brother travelled in his carriage, accompanied by R. Isaac, son-in-law of R. Moses, a member of the community. They went to Brody, and brought about an agreement with the Elders of the Four Lands, under which the community of Bolechow was to pay 1,300 gulden every year for three years. The Elders said: "If you are prepared to pay in cash 1,200 gulden for the present year, you will have a receipt and will be absolved from payment of the balance of this year's amount." Hearing this, R. Isaac, my brother's companion, induced him to advance the money in order that they might share the profit of 100 gulden between them. He knew that my brother carried a considerable sum of money on him to exchange it for imperial money, and particularly for ducats, which were then valued at the rate of 19 gulden. But he proved a bad counsellor.

After my brother had proceeded to Brody an order came from the new bishop of Lemberg, Sierakowski,[1] to close the Holy Synagogue, which remained closed from the Passover to the Feast of Weeks. I settled this affair for a sum of 20 ducats paid out of my own pocket, after which I procured a license to open the synagogue, written and signed by the bishop; this license is still in my hands.

It further happened that there were no weighing machines in our town, the old ones having been destroyed in the fire. So I bought a large iron bar, 125 Brabant lb. in weight.[2] It is of the true weight, and is in use to this day in our community. Year after year it is lent out, and one Polish *grosz* is paid for every stone of goods

[1] Correctly the archbishop Wenceslaus Hieronymus Sierakowski.

[2] It is not clear what the author means by "iron bar" and "iron weighing-machine". An iron bar would suggest a "steel-yard", which would not weigh 125 lb., but would register a weight of 125 lb.

weighed. The weighing machine and the measure for honey are to this day in the hands of the treasurer of the lease-office. The members of the Guild of Shopkeepers, that is, the traders dealing in all kinds of goods, declared this machine to be correct. These shopkeepers always meet during the intermediate days of the Feast of Tabernacles to elect the Elders, Managers and other officials of their Guild. On the eighth day of Tabernacles they usually arrange a banquet. The fee for every stone of goods weighed and for every pot of honey measured was fixed by the Guild at half a *kreuzer*. The weighing-machine was lent out for at least 150 gulden yearly. I myself paid for the iron weighing-machine 15 ducats and for the copper measure 2 ducats.

It was on account of these expenses that the cash necessary for the purchase of Hungarian wine became so short. The Elders of our community could not return us our money, and they were not aware of the increasing wrong which was done to us.

Now the chief of the community, R. Israel, son of R. Naḥman, was about to travel to Hungary to collect his debts at Nagybanya for the ox-hides which his clerk had sold on credit for a sum of several hundred ducats. As the time for payment approached, R. Israel himself proceeded thither to collect the money. I learned that he had also the idea of purchasing Hungarian wines. So I asked him if he would be willing to follow my advice concerning his intended purchases. R. Israel agreed and promised to act in accordance with my instructions. So I advised him to ride on his horse to Tarczal, where he should stay in the house of R. Ensil Kaz, a German Jew, and await my coming for seven days. "Then", I continued, "we will buy wines that should be to your advantage." R. Israel did so, and rode to Tarczal, where he met R. Hirsch, son of R. Elijah, — also known as R. Hirsch Koristower, — who was sent by R. Hirsch Duliber of Skole with an order to purchase new wines. This R. Hirsch Koristower had already acquired from the noble Patay 100 casks of the new vintage, on condition, however, that the dry grapes, which were as sweet as raisins, should not be picked and trodden and pressed together with moist grapes. The price paid for these 100 casks was 700 ducats. R. Hirsch made it a condition of the purchase that he himself should be present and see how the Gentile servants pressed the fruit with their naked feet, which had been bathed in wine made for the consumption of people of their own faith.

R. Hirsch, son of Elijah, when he met R. Israel, boasted to him that he had bought the 100 casks from the nobleman Patay, whereupon R. Israel said: "I would rather buy ritual wine, and I have no wish for other wine;" for R. Israel had then begun to practise piety.[1] Then R. Hirsch said: "There is a Jew here called R. Loeb of Dobromil, and another R. Ber Terkil, also a man of means." R. Israel said: "There is also a German Jew here, R. Ensil, with whom I have to speak and to make acquaintance." Immediately R. Ensil Kaz was informed of this, and the three formed a partnership, that is, R, Ensil, R. Loeb and R. Ber. They sold R. Israel 30 casks of new wine, at 8 ducats per cask, on condition that one *put*[2] of dry grapes should be put into each cask. On the very day of his arrival at Tarczal R. Hirsch was busy arranging the price between the (three) partners and R. Israel. The partners received as earnest money 80 ducats, called Banya-ducats,[3] new and "warm" from the mint at Banya, where they were coined. The remainder, 160 ducats, R. Israel arranged to pay on receipt of the wares, because in the process of fermentation the wine leaks out from the casks, and the casks must, therefore, remain in the cellars on the spot until the wine becomes clear of sediment, and then they can be moved.

[1] An allusion to R. Israel's adherence to the Ḥasidic movement?
[2] A measure of capacity, nearly a Polish quart as standardised in the eighteenth century.
[3] Correctly Körmöczbanya or Kremnitz. The author uses both forms of the name.

Now we can see how many mistakes were made by R. Israel, son of R. Naḥman, in this affair, acting on the bad advice of R. Hirsch, son of R. Elijah. First, R. Hirsch bought 100 casks of wine, each costing 7 ducats, which was terribly dear, as I will relate further in its place. We bought better wines from the vine-yards of the Empress and from nobles who had very fine vine-yards on the hill sides, and did not pay more than 4 or 5 ducats per cask, whilst R. Hirsch paid 7 ducats per cask for moist grapes, that is, almost half as much again as he should have paid. Then R. Hirsch misled R. Israel and made him pay three quarters of his money for nothing. He paid 8 ducats for a thing worth at the most two ducats, for the ritual wine, which R. Israel purchased from the partners, was grown in the vine-yards of the poor wine-growers, situated in the flat country, the grapes from which are not sweet and are therefore cheap. A cask of such wine costs 5 Hungarian gulden or 15 marks, or a maximum of 7 *vansh* or 21 *maryash*.[1]

After this had been settled my brother, Aryeh Loeb, and myself arrived in Tarczal. R. Israel was ashamed of himself for not having followed our advice and for having purchased wines without our knowledge. The partners who sold the wines asked me not to find fault with the price R. Israel had paid, and they promised us 3 casks of choice ritual wine, which they in fact brought us. I sealed the casks at once. R. Israel was mindful of the promise he made me at Lemberg during his transactions with the Gentile Solski about the ox-hides, when I obtained credit for him and helped him to obtain a reasonable price. He had then promised me a gold coin of 5 ducats. Now he fulfilled his promise and gave me 5 Hungarian ducats, presenting me moreover with two small, very handsome pistols. On this occasion I recalled the saying of our Sages: "When a man has made a bad bargain, he should

---

[1] *Mariash* were 20 kreuzer pieces. Concerning *vansh* I have been unable to find any information.

not be told so to his face." [1] It was better for us to keep
silence and to receive three casks of good wine, fit for
Kiddush and *Habdalah*.[2]

The year 561 (1761) was a year of wonderful vintage.
Wine was plentiful and very good; but we could not buy
any, because the new wine was unsuitable for our retail
business, being too sweet to drink before it had matured.
Older wines were very scarce, and I was afraid that they
would become very dear; and we had not enough ready
money to buy the wine which we needed to sell in Lemberg. So I used to pray devoutly every morning and
every evening, saying, "we will cast our lot upon the
Lord. He will send us deliverance from his heaven in his
loving-kindness." [3]

Passing through the market at Tarczal, I met a Hun-
ungarian[4], formerly in the service of Count Buttler,[5] who
had a house there. He knew us quite well, because
we used to buy wines from the Count's cellar. He told
me that he had now been appointed inspector of the
Crown Estates, and that the wine vaults of the Crown
were now under his management. He asked if my brother,
Aryeh Loeb, was there, and on my replying in the affir-
mative, said: "If you wish to buy good wines, we have
in our cellars 280 casks of prime quality of last year."
I went with him at once to the wine-vaults, tasted the
wine, and found it suitable. Then I informed my brother,
who went to see the inspector. I told my brother that
it would be advisable to make a selection of 100 casks,
and I went to the house of Kegler, the inspector. We
settled the price at 350 ducats for 100 casks, and we paid
100 ducats at once; the remaining 250 ducats were to be

---

[1] Keth, 17 a.

[2] Benedictions said on Friday evening and on the conclusion of the Sabbath.

[3] Paraphrase of Psalm 55, 23.

[4] In the original "Marsi" — perhaps miswritten "Magyar"? His name
was Kegler, as we learn from the further narrative of Ber.

[5] A German family which migrated into Hungary, and the head of which
assumed the Hungarian title of Count.

paid at the Feast of St. John, that is, in *Tammuz* 522 (1762). We purchased besides this 20 casks of good wine from a Greek at Tarczal for 60 ducats, and 15 casks more for 45 ducats from the Gentile surgeon at Tarczal. So with the little money we had, through the blessing of God, we procured a considerable stock to meet the needs of our business. We brought it to Lemberg and obtained good prices for it; but we lost on the exchange, because the ducat was worth only 27 gulden at that time. The remainder of the purchase price, 250 ducats, was paid, as arranged, on the Feast of St. John, having been sent to Tarczal by a special messenger.

In the same year, 521 (1761), I arranged the marriage of my son Joseph with his first wife, the worthy Hannah, daughter of the excellent scholar R. Joseph,[1] son of R. Jacob Koppel, generally known as R. Koppel the Fat. R. Joseph was son-in-law of the Gaon R. Isaac, Rabbi at Monasteryscze, who in his turn was the son-in-law of R. Abraham, son of R. Kalman, deputy to the Council of Four Lands from Tysmienica. This R. Isaac was afterwards appointed to be Rabbi at Tysmienica, where he died after holding office for nine years.

In 1762 my brother and I proceeded to Tarczal, where the three partners I have spoken of offered us 90 casks of wine of a much better quality than that which had been purchased the previous year by R. Israel, who had then paid the unprecedented price of 8 ducats for a wine which was but grape-juice. We selected 40 casks and paid 5 ducats per cask. Later we took the remainder, 50 casks, for 4 ducats each. This bargain being struck, the merchants were going to purchase a fresh stock of 140 casks from a Hungarian noble, and they asked me to make the choice for them. I went to the noble's cellar, and chose from among 200 casks 140 casks of good wine, leaving the poorer quality there. It was then that I came upon one of the officials

---

[1] See p. 84. R. Joseph was one of R. Ber's friends during his sojourn in Tysmienica.

of the Crown vaults, who had sold me last year 100
casks of old wine. He said: "Why don't you call on us
to taste our wines? We have a large stock now of 500
casks of excellent quality, nearly 100 of them containing
máslás." I went with him and saw them; and in truth, the
cellars were full of excellent brands. I discussed the matter
with my brother, and reminded him of what the Priest
Wieniawski, the owner of Bolechow, used to say: "If God
sends another good year for the wine, I myself will go
to Hungary to buy some." We then went to the house
of the inspector, Kegler, who knew that my brother was
friendly with the Priest, and we said: "We want to buy
some wines from the Crown cellars for the Priest Wieniawski, who is a friend of yours." Kegler then made an
arrangement with the other officials, according to which
we were to choose our wines — 200 casks — and to seal
them with our seal. In two months we were to send
100 ducats with an agreement signed by us or by the
Priest for 200 casks of wine for the sum of 1000 ducats.
We were allowed to take away 100 casks with us at once.
In half a year's time we were to send 500 ducats more,
and would then be entitled to take the remaining casks.
There would still remain a debt of 400 ducats, which
would have to be paid in another half-year.

Our brother-in-law, R. Aaron, was just then staying at
Miskolcz with his brother-in-law, R. Elieser, from Zurawno.
As they did not find any wine worth buying, they sent
me a letter by a messenger asking me to inform them if
there was anything to be done at Tarczal. I told them
the truth — that many good sorts were to be found there.
They then came to Tarczal and purchased as much as
they needed. When we took away our wine from there,
they remained in our debt, the one for 6 ducats and the
other for 5 ducats. Until today they have not paid this
debt, as is proved by their bond, which is in my hands.

We carried our wine to Munkacs, where we were met
by our brother, R. Seeb Wolf, who gave us 200 ducats
for the cost of transport, and told us that Wieniawski, the

owner of Bolechow, had died. So I was compelled to send a
special messenger with a letter to the three merchants at
Tarczal, telling them to do everything to obtain the wine
I had chosen from the Crown cellars, and warning them
urgently not to act otherwise. They followed my advice
and bought the wine, having told the inspector Kegler
of the death of his friend Wieniawski, and they entered
into a further agreement with the officials of the Crown,
to take half of the whole store, that is, 250 casks, paying
100 ducats more. They explained this to me in their
answer to my letter, which they wrote to me at that time.
Besides those wines the three merchants purchased many
others, and their partnership lasted three years. Up to
the end of their partnership I acted as the accountant
in their business, and I examined their documents, as I
shall explain in its time and place, the Lord willing.

We carried our wine, more than 100 casks, to Lemberg,
leaving 40 casks at Stryi. The noble Deszert, the new
owner of Bolechow — Wieniawski, the previous landlord,
having died — bought 4 casks from us. I spoke to him
about the business in Hungarian wine, reminding him that
Wieniawski had been very interested in the wine trade,
having made a great deal of money in that business; and
Deszert was willing to do some business through me. But
it happened that R. Sender, the beadle of the community
of Stryi, the confidential agent of this noble, reported it to
R. Isaac, son-in-law of R. Moses, a member of our community. R. Isaac was a great enemy of mine, without any
other reason than envy, so he did all that he could to
dissuade the landlord from doing any business with me.

The wine we had purchased was of a good vintage, but
too sweet for immediate use. Everywhere there was plenty
of wine on the market, but no buyer for it. I was engaged
that year in the building of my house, and my brother,
Aryeh Loeb, was finishing his house, which had been
begun the year before: all that of course required
money. The time was approaching for going to Hungary,
and there was no money at our disposal to pay our debts

from the last year for the wine which we had stored at
Lemberg and Stryi. However, the Lord pitied us and sent
the cure before the plague.

None of the vintage bought by R. Israel, son of R. Naḥman, was sold up to the third year; he had purchased
that wine at a very high price. In order to console himself, therefore, R. Israel started a new venture — the exchange of gulden at the town of Banya, in Hungary. I
heard about it during the journey he made in 521 (1761)
to Banya to collect the debts for the ox-hides, on the
occasion when I had asked him to go to Tarczal, which
he promised to do. I then recalled an experience of my
youth, when, living at Tysmienica, I was occupied in
dealing with silver and gold. Near the abode of my
father-in-law there lived at that time a true neighbour,
a gold and silver smith by profession, named R. Joseph,
son of R. Isaiah, the *ḥazzan* of the community at Tysmienica (in his later years R. Joseph was also appointed
to be *ḥazzan* of the community). This goldsmith knew
how to clean silver and to refine gold. We used to exchange the old gulden and other good coins too, and
to send them to Breslau, which was then under the
rule of the Austrian Emperor; we always received at the
office of the Emperor's mint, which was in that place,
good money, all straightforward without any deception.

Following my advice, R. Israel took with him 50 gulden
of various sorts, called *"Keplech"*, *"Pintlech"*, *"Hitlech"*
and *"Fonwer"*,[1] and other coins containing much pure
silver. During his stay at Banya R. Israel showed these
coins to the masters of the mint, who were German
goldsmiths, but neither could he make himself understood
by them, nor could the masters make R. Israel understand;
thus he did nothing in the money business. I then had
to write out for every coin its equivalent in German,
and my letter, together with the coins, was sent through

[1] These names do not occur in the literature of the numismatics of the
eighteenth century; they sound like Yiddish.

R. Benjamin, son of R. Kalman Kaz, to the masters of the mint at Banya. This messenger returned with a statement giving the exact value of each gulden in the various groups. After that many of our brethren besides R. Israel became eager to search for and to collect gulden and rare coins. R. Isaac, son-in-law of R. Moses, joined him in partnership, and they spent large sums out of their own pockets in the money-changing business. Both members of this firm agreed to lend us 446 ducats until the Fairs which were due to be held at Lemberg in the month of *Tebet*, in 523 (17th December 1762 — 15th January 1763).

I myself proceeded to Hungary, whilst my brother remained at Lemberg to collect the debts and to sell the wine stored there and at Stryi. Our employee, Joseph, son of R. Samuel Lukwitser, rode to the town of Banya to receive the 446 ducats from the agents of the money-changers. I made the journey on a good horse, and a peasant from a village near Skole accompanied me leading another horse, for I had then bought two good horses from a nobleman. I arrived safely at Tarczal, and all the people were glad to see me come. On the way there I bought two large pikes, which astonished the people who saw me bringing these fish. They said to me: "The luck of the fish will bring you luck."

When the members of the wine firm at Tarczal heard that I had to await there my employee Joseph with the bulk of the money, they approached me with the request that I should look into their business accounts already described. Each brought his papers and registers and laid them on the table in my room, which was covered with them. I sat down to read these documents and to find out from the whole and from each document in particular the figures showing the purchase of the wines, the expenses involved and the particulars of the sale. After five days spent in investigating and examining those papers I found out the proper way to put their accounts in order. They had in fact carried on their business for

more than three years. They had bought over 1000 casks
of wine, which had been stored in twenty wine-cellars
and had been sold retail for different amounts. I made
out a report as to all the purchases of the wines; the
number of casks and their value; the different brands;
from which Gentile producer they had been bought;
and in which cellar they had been stored. Another report
referred to the sales, showing to whom the wines had
been sold and for what amount. Further I noted all the
expenses incurred in the transport of the wines to their
destination, and also how much had leaked out from every
cask, the quantity being one cask a month for every 100
casks, which is a factor to be taken into account by all
wine traders. After the calculation had been made there
were still 20 casks unaccounted for, and nobody knew
who had taken them or emptied them. After deduction
of all the losses and heavy expenses, there remained
for the firm a net profit of 2100 ducats, which divided
into three parts gave to each partner 700 ducats. The
partners remunerated me for my trouble in putting their
accounts in order with two casks of ritual wine, of the
variety called *máslás*.

I acquired 50 casks of *máslás* from this firm and 45 casks
of a good sort from the Greek merchant, but I was still
looking for old wines. I found, however, in the cellars
of Count Buttler among 80 casks of *máslás* only 10 casks
of an old wine, which had lost its sweetness. The price
of this sort was 25 ducats the cask, as the official of the
Count in Tarczal had told me, but the remaining 10 casks
were to be sold for 16 ducats each. I said to the official:
"If the Count is disposed to sell, I will take this poorer
wine." The official accordingly wrote to the Count, who
came to Tarczal and spoke with me; and we settled the
price. I was to take 7 casks for 70 ducats. As I had
already spent the bulk of my ready cash in purchases
of wine, I had to make up the balance in goods of
equal value, so the Count took from me the two horses,
representing a value of 30 ducats, and the remaining

40 ducats were made up with fancy goods, silver and gold watches, handsome snuff-boxes and valuable Mechlin laces.

About that time I entered into a contract with a merchant, one M. Ronsanet, a Frenchman, a wholesale dealer well-known in the countries of Europe. He had pledged himself to furnish the King of Poland and Elector of Saxony, Augustus II,[1] with all sorts of wine which are to be found in the countries and provinces of Europe. Ronsanet made an agreement with me, under which I was to provide him with barrels of Tokay wine called *Ausbruch*, of the sort which is used in Vienna at the Emperor's court. I purchased for him at Tokay ten barrels of good wine, and brought them to Lemberg, whence they were sent to Dresden. Thus I fulfilled my engagement, having delivered to the Frenchman wines for the articles I have just enumerated, which articles he gave me as earnest money when we entered into the contract. We managed to sell our wines as usual.

At that time the High Tribunal, which had had its seat for many hundred years at Lublin, was transferred to Lemberg. This Tribunal was the Supreme Court over all the Courts which existed in each *starostaship*.[2] Each province and district used to elect a number of wealthy noblemen, learned in the law, who assembled at Warsaw, the capital of Poland, and there the Diet chose from among them men known for their high character, fear of God, love of truth and incorruptibility, and sent them to Lublin to attend there the sessions of the Supreme Court, which now however was transferred to Lemberg.[3] Each candidate had to be elected by the unanimous vote of the

[1] Correctly Augustus III.

[2] See p. 67, note 2.

[3] At the Convocation (or Pre-election) Diet of 1764 it was decided to divide the High Tribunal at Lublin into two sections — one for Great Poland and the other for Little Poland. The sessions of the latter section of the Court were held alternately at Lublin and Lemberg. This lasted till 1768. See Stanislaw Kutrzeba, *History of the Polish Constitution* (P.), 3 d edition, vol. I, 1905, p. 257. Ber refers to the first session of the Court at Lemberg.

nobles in his district or *voyevodship*;[1] for under the Polish Constitution one single person could stop the proceedings of an Assembly, and every affair, trifling or important, had to be settled with the consent of all members of the Assembly,[2] particularly in legal matters, which indeed are the very foundation of the State.

So the deputies to the Supreme Court, great and powerful noblemen, came to Lemberg; and the deputy from the district of Lublin, a man of great wealth, took up his residence in a house of stone, the property of the Carmelite friars, where we also stayed. This deputy tasted our wine, and chose a cask from the old ones which I had purchased from Count Buttler at Tarczal, paying 35 Hungarian ducats for the upper half of the cask, whilst the lower part with the sediment was left with us. After the clear half of the wine had been taken I filled the barrel with a wine of good quality, and sold it to *Pani* Kossakowska, the widow of the Castellan of Kaminsk, for 40 ducats.

The remainder of the old wines from the purchase made from Count Buttler was sold retail in bottles at one ducat a quart. 180 bottles were bought by the Governor and Chief Commander of the garrison of Lemberg, the noble Senal, a Frenchman, and a great expert in all kinds of wine. His cellars always contained an assortment of various wines from all the countries of Europe. When the Commander and other nobles whom he invited to dinner tasted the wine from the bottles, they all wondered how it was that there was such a very agreeable aroma, and he asked me to come to his house. He took me into his room and said: "My good Sir, tell me what you have done to those bottles of wine that you sold me, that they have such a pleasant aroma."

---

[1] This statement of Ber's is quite correct. See Kutrzeba, *op. cit.*, p. 209. But no corroboration is to be found for Ber's statement that the Diet at Warsaw appointed the members of the Supreme Court from among the candidates elected in the districts.

[2] See Introduction, p. 19.

I replied: "Believe me, Sir, I do not know anything about doctoring wine. As I buy it I sell it. I bought this wine in casks, bottled it, and sold it as it was — nothing more." Thus I stopped his enquiries and left his house in peace; but he was very put out that I did not reveal to him the secret, which is as follows. It happened that Ornalt, the bookkeeper of the French tradesman, Ronsanet, when he first came from Dresden to Lemberg with various sorts of wine, showed me some Spanish wine bottled in small half-quart bottles, looking like Provençal oil. When I tasted this wine I noticed an extraordinarily fine aroma, and realised at once what a flavour this would give to a Hungarian wine. So I used always to buy some bottles of that Spanish wine, and to add half a wine-glass-full to a quart bottle of Hungarian wine. The price of the Spanish wine was one ducat for four small half-quart bottles.

In that year 524 (1764) I arranged the marriage of my son, R. Joseph, with a girl of 11 years, Hannah, daughter of R. Joseph of Tysmienica. Her grandfather, R. Isaac,[1] Rabbi in Tysmienica, brought her into my house on the first day of Nisan, 524 (3rd April 1764). The wedding was a very splendid affair. The venerable Gaon, R. Ḥayyim Cohen Rapaport, presented the bridegroom with a learned address written and signed by his holy hand, which reached us before the ceremony. The grandfather of the bride was greatly pleased when he saw "the house of my precious things",[2] and found that I was a man of substance. He thanked the Almighty that his grandchild was given to reliable people.

At that time Frederick William,[3] King of Prussia, conquered the Province of Silesia. Polish merchants used to take to Silesia all the best silver coins they had from the time of the late kings, and also the new gulden

---

[1] See p. 118.
[2] Is. 39².
[3] Should be Frederick the Great.

coined in the days of Augustus III, King of Poland and
Elector of Saxony,[1] because goods could be bought at
Breslau and Frankfurt only for ready money. When the
King of Prussia learned that great sums of money were
thus brought in from Poland, he at once ordered Polish
gulden to be coined, stamped with the image and the
superscription of the Polish King. These coins were
made in Prussia from the Polish coins received from
Polish buyers, some of which were handed to the masters
of the mint, who (broke up the coins and) made new gulden. But these gulden minted by order of the King of
Prussia were worth, according to the silver they contained, $7^{1}/_{2}$ kreuzer, and some of those minted at a later
date were worth only 5 kreuzer, while the gulden of
the Polish Crown were always worth 19 kreuzer. As a
result, the value of the ducat increased, and it was bought
and exchanged for 27 gulden. Thus all goods in Poland
became dearer, including wine; a cask of ordinary wine,
which was previously sold for 15 ducats at most, rose to 18.
All this, however, did not cover the loss one had to incur
in buying gold coins at a high price.[2]

We travelled in 524 (1764) to Hungary and purchased
in the locality of Tarczal 80 casks of ordinary shop wine,
from the cellars of Count Karolyi, at 5 ducats per cask,
besides other sorts of wine which we bought retail at
high prices, for the good máslás was already sold, and
whatever was left was dear. We returned to Lemberg
and sold all we could, but much remained unsold; and
my brother, R. Aryeh Loeb, had to stay at Lemberg
to dispose of the rest. Another brother, R. Wolf, went
with me to Hungary in the month of Marḥeshvan, 525
(27th October — 25th November 1764). We stopped at
Tarczal, but we could not obtain any choice wine there,
and the ordinary sorts in the cellars of the Crown were

---

[1] Minted in Saxony, but not in Poland. See Introduction, p. 26.

[2] See Introduction as regards the devaluation of Polish money in the
eighteenth century.

also all sold. So I had to buy ordinary wine from the
cellars of the noble Patay and from Count Karolyi, altogether about 80 casks, and the other wines I bought
from some other wine-producers. I had to send my
brother Wolf to Miskolcz, as I thought that he might
find some good *máslás* there. He bought thirty casks,
but they were no better than those we had purchased
at Tarczal. My brother returned . . .

. . . His skin sack was full of money. I caught hold
of the sack and took it before I seized the thief. I put
away the money on one side, caught the thief with both
my hands, and called the people of the house, but they
were all asleep. The Gentile guard got up and lit
a light, and then all the others appeared. The thief began
to beg me not to hand him over to the Gentiles who
were then staying in our house, namely, a nobleman with
many attendants. In order not to put a fellow-Jew to
shame in the eyes of Gentiles, we decided to punish his
theft with the lash, for he had not the money to pay
double what he had stolen, as is prescribed by our holy
Torah. My brother consented to this judgement. The thief
was placed on the ground, and two servants held him
by his hands and feet, while I gave him thirty-nine strokes
with thongs made of calf leather. The thief then immediately fled from Lemberg, and did not return to his
home at Dolina; and to this day nothing further has been
heard of him.

The proceeds of the sale of our wine having been considerable, we decided to go to Hungary to purchase more
wine. In the month of *Adar*, in 525 (22nd February —
23rd March 1765), I departed from Bolechow, and arrived
at Tarczal just before the Passover. I stayed with R. Ensil
Kaz, whom I have previously mentioned. Good wines were
not to be obtained, and the ordinary sorts too had
been all sold. The eve of the Passover arrived, and there
came to R. Ensil his brother-in-law, R. Ezekiel, from the

village of Szerencs,[1] and with him his son's tutor, the learned R. Isaac of Przeworsk. He pressed me to go and spend the Festival in his house, in order to perform the ceremony of circumcision on his son on the second day of the Passover, which was the eighth day since the birth of the child. R. Ensil and his wife were very upset that I was not going to stay at their house during the Festival; but they consented, though unwillingly, to my going to perform the ceremony of circumcision on their nephew (for R. Ezekiel's wife was the sister of Serl, the wife of R. Ensil). R. Ezekiel had no other choice, for when he went to Mad[2] none of the *Mohels* — although there were many there, because it was a large place — wanted to leave his home and spend the two first nights of the Festival away. So R. Ezekiel had to come to Tarczal and urge his brother-in-law, R. Ensil, and his wife to let me go. Accordingly I joined R. Ezekiel. We travelled in my carriage, with four horses, and my clerk, Joseph, and the Gentile servant went with me. R. Ezekiel lodged and fed us all, and the horses, for four days; and as soon as we arrived he told my clerk to go into the wine cellar and to choose a cask of a nice wine for my own use. We remained there the two first days of the Passover and the first of the intermediate days. On the second of these days there arrived R. Ezekiel's friends from all the localities and villages in the neighbourhood of Szerencs, more than fifty people of consequence. R. Ezekiel arranged the meal, which follows the circumcision, on the third day after the ceremony was performed;[3] I had to attend this ceremonial banquet during the whole day.

This R. Ezekiel, at that time the lease-holder of the village of Szerencs, was the father of the Rabbi Isaac Eisik of Nagy Kallo, in Hungary. When I spent the

---

[1] In the county of Zemplen.

[2] In the same county.

[3] *I. e.* on the fourth day of the Passover, Tuesday, the 10th of April. A banquet for those who attend a circumcision is part of the regular ceremonial.

Passover in his father's house R. Eisik was a pretty little boy, who played and sang with a pleasant voice. When he grew up his singing made him famous among the *Ḥasidim*, as it is said: "Sing unto the Lord a new song and His praise in the congregation of the saints." [1] R. Eisik's first wife was a daughter of R. Ensil, just mentioned, and their mothers were sisters. R. Eisik became famous throughout the country on account of his piety. He was diligent in the study of rabbinical authors, and became a Rabbi and teacher in Israel; to this day he is Chief of the *Beth Din* in Nagy Kallo. [2]

After the Passover, towards the end of the month of *Nisan*, I learned of 80 casks of wine ready for sale by the owner of the village of Monok. [3] "And, behold, the time of singing of birds is come" [4] — the wedding-day of R. Ensil's son, the youth Jacob, who married an orphan-girl, the daughter of the late R. Judah Loeb of Kallo. The wedding was arranged to take place in the house of the bride's uncle, the well-known R. Eisik of Kallo, who then held the lease of the village of Monok, where those 80 casks of wine were available. I had to come to this wedding with them with my carriage and horses. On arriving there I immediately tasted all the wines and purchased 60 casks, which proved to be good. I also bought 40 casks from the landlord of Szerencs, the noble Almasi, and some more wine at Tarczal, and carried the whole purchase, altogether 120 casks, to Lemberg.

[1] Ps. 149[1]. The word translated "saints" is *ḥasidim*.

[2] Isaac Eisik Taub, whom our author has in mind, was born in 1751 at Nagy Kallo. He went to Poland, where he completed his rabbinical studies. In 1781 he was elected to fill the post of Rabbi in his native town, which post he occupied till his death, in 1821. He was very popular among Hungarian Jewry, and many stories were current in connection with his name and activities. His Hungarian Poem "The Bird" is still sung by Hungarian Jews on festivals. — I am obliged for these few biographical items to the Hebrew scholar, Leopold Grünwald, of Budapest.

[3] Situated in the county of Zemplen, in the district of Szerencs.

[4] Sing of Songs 2[12].

In that year[1] commenced the second session of the Supreme Court or High Tribunal. But the nobles who attended this session were not so wealthy as those who came to the first. Then all the nobles and judges were dressed in garments of Neapolitan silk, but now they wore simple silk made at Tours. They also demanded cheaper wine for their drink. At the third session the members of the Court appeared in garments of serge, a mixture of wool and flax, very poor and humble. Shortly afterwards the Court closed because of the rebellion of the Polish people against their King Poniatowski, as I shall have to mention in its place.

In that year 525 (1765), the estates of Bolechow and its surroundings were sold to Count Joachim Potocki, the Cup-Bearer of Lithuania, for a sum of 1,200.000 gulden, by Prince Poninski,[2] son-in-law of Prince Lubomirski, our previous landlord, who died in the same year in which the martyr R. Moses was killed in the town of Rzeszow, as I have related above.[3] After the death of the said Lubomirski his son, the Starosta of Bohuslaw,[4] inherited the property of Bolechow. Before a year was out he also passed away, and then the old Prince's wife, a German lady,[5] held the estates as regent. When her sons grew up the inheritance was divided between them, and Bolechow passed into the hands of Prince Adolf Lubomirski.[6] He

---

[1] Omitted in the MS. Apparently 1765.

[2] Prince Adam Poninski, who was later appointed to be State Treasurer, and became notorious through the charge of peculation brought against him in 1790.

[3] Not preserved in the MS.

[4] Prince George Lubomirski. Bohuslaw is to-day a township in the Province of Kiev.

[5] Her maiden name was Stein. She was the second wife of George Lubomirski. Cf. A. Boniecki and A. Rejski, *Polish Heraldry* (P.), s. v. Lubomirski. Here as often elsewhere the author of the Memoirs shows a detailed knowledge of the family connections of the Polish nobility, which makes his anecdotes a valuable source for the social history of the eighteenth century.

[6] There were three sons, Adolf, George and Francis, and a daughter, Josepha, the wife of Poninski. See the work on *Polish Heraldry* quoted in the previous note.

used to play cards with the nobles at Warsaw, and lost the large sum of 600,000 gulden. He mortgaged the property of Bolechow for that amount to the winner, but his brother-in-law, Prince Poninski, paid his debts and took over the estate. Prince Poninski's steward, Hadziewicz, then prepared a register of the revenues brought in by the town, the villages and the salt-springs, and brought it to his master at Lemberg. Up to then the income had not amounted to more then 50,000 gulden, but the steward showed it in his register as 74,000 gulden per annum. Poninski, who was a great scoundrel, met Count Joachim Potocki at Lemberg, and sold him the property for 1,200.000 gulden, which was double the price it had fetched at the two previous sales (to Count Poniatowski and to Prince Lubomirski).[1]

When the new landlord noticed how high a price had been paid for this property, he ordered his steward, Bobrowski, to go to Bolechow and to find out the easiest way to increase the revenue of the estate. My brother, Aryeh Loeb, was then with me at Lemberg, engaged in the wine business. The steward Bobrowski, when he arrived at Bolechow, was eager to meet an educated and intelligent Jew. But God wished to punish some of our community. A Jew named Ḥayyim, son of R. Joshua, a poor man full of envy and hatred for his fellows, appeared before the steward, and, perceiving that his aim was only to rob, played the informer, and told him that all the people of Bolechow were very wealthy men; that more than 200 families were hiring rooms in the houses of others; and that all of them were exceedingly rich, the least of them being worth 20,000 gulden. The steward believed R. Ḥayyim's story, and thought of the following plan. His master (Count Potocki) had bought on his advice several villages near the town of Brzezan, the so-called

---

[1] One feature more to illustrate the bad character of Poninski, whom R. Nisbet Bain, in his *The Last King of Poland* (London, 1907), p. 76 styles "hireling of Russia, scoundrel and swindler."

estates of Kurdan,[1] and had paid a very high price for them. The steward reported to his master on the Jews who hired rooms at Bolechow, and they decided to remove these people to the village of Wysokie[2] and to build houses for them there, with the idea that when the population of Wysokie increased, it would receive the privileges of a town. The people of Bolechow did not, however, wish to go from their home, where they were born and bred.

At first the steward tried to persuade our people with soft words and great promises; but when he saw that his efforts were unavailing, he began arresting them and compelling them to pay out of their own pockets many hundreds of gulden towards the building of houses in the new town. Some of our people suffered great hardships, and none of the whole of our community could help them, for nobody understood Polish or could speak it fluently and correctly like a man of intelligence; and only such a man could gain a hearing and refute the calumnies of those wicked men who curried favour with the nobles by telling lies against their fellow-Jews and causing them to be robbed of their property.

Then there came to the steward, Bobrowski, R. Abraham, son of R. Michel, a native of Nawarya,[3] and a member of our community, who had built a new house in Bolechow, and said: "I am willing to go to live in the new place, Podwysokie, on condition that the landlord will order a new house to be built there exactly similar to the one I have here at Bolechow." The steward agreed to this, and assured R. Abraham on his honour that a handsome building would be erected. "They are," he said, "already building some fine houses there. Possibly one already built will suit you, and if so you will have the first choice." R. Abraham accordingly left his house here

[1] Perhaps Kurdwanowka, now in the district of Buczacz in Galicia?
[2] Correctly Podwysokie, (as it is called below), now in the district of Buczacz.
[3] Small place in the district of Lemberg.

at Bolechow to the treasury of the landlord, and removed
to the new place, where he took up his abode and lived
for many years with his wife and only son, R. Michel.

The steward Bobrowski, seeing that R. Abraham was so
eager to go to the new town, again attempted to persuade
the people of our community to go and to live there along
with R. Abraham. Those who would not be persuaded
he ordered to be imprisoned, treated violently, tormented
and coerced by heavy extortions, until some of our people
were compelled to pay out of their own pockets many
hundred gulden for the building of their houses in the
new town. Nevertheless, the steward was not satisfied.
He came down to the town[1] and took up his residence
in my house. I had there a synagogue, established out of
respect for my aged father, then ninety years old, the
learned R. Judah, for being weak on his feet he could not
attend service at the synagogue of the community every
day. I, therefore, devoted the three rooms on the top of
the house to a synagogue, where a *minyan*[2] said prayers
with my old father; and when the Bishop of Lemberg,
Sierakowski, granted a licence for the synagogue of our
community, I got him to issue a licence to my father
allowing him to perform his devotions with a *minyan*
in a room set aside for public worship. But the steward
Bobrowski paid no attention to this; he dispersed the
minyan and made a prison of the holy place wherein to
detain those who would not listen to his deceiving lies.

Everyone can imagine what great grief, anxiety and
distress the members of our community suffered when
they were forced to leave their native place, which is
against nature, for it is said: "The charm of a place is
with the inhabitants".[3] These trials lasted for half a year,
until my brother, R. Aryeh Loeb, returned home to spend
the Passover. He heard of the bitter and cruel wrongs

---

[1] Apparently from the castle.

[2] *Minyan* (Heb., = "number") is used to mean the minimum number
of ten male worshippers required for a full service.

[3] Sotah, 47 a.

committed by the steward on our people, and, although
no member of our family had suffered — for, on the
contrary, Bobrowski had always behaved towards us as
a good friend — my brother said to him: "Sir, think what
you are doing to the people! Will it please the landowner
that you extract from the inhabitants of his town the
wealth they have amassed through their labour? The landlord's subjects are poor, naked and lacking in everything,
and therefore the revenues of the owner, which depend
on the population of the town, will surely be diminished.
I have always heard that one tries to increase the income
of estates from the timber of the forests, from the rivers
and lakes, from the produce of the soil; but from the
helpless tenants —!" My brother said more to the same
purpose in his pleasant and intelligent way, speaking
sincerely from the depths of a heart which was always
zealous for the good of our community; and his words
touched the steward's heart and softened his determination.
Everyone was released from prison, and the steward did
not force anyone else of our community to settle in the
new town except the above-mentioned R. Abraham, son
of R. Michel, who continued to live in his new house there
for many years in poverty and privation. His house at
Bolechow, which he had exchanged for that in the new
town, was soon sold to one R. Loeb of Nyniow[1] who had
come to live in our town. This R. Loeb, together with
some partners, people of our community, had to lease
some of the revenues of the town at a heavy price. He
had come to our place to seek the protection of our landlord against his former lords, and did all our owner wanted
him to do. This R. Loeb acquired the house of R. Abraham for 80 ducats. However, before the year of the lease
(of the revenues) ran out, R. Loeb made peace with his
former landlord and fled from our town, abandoning the
house and taking with him a considerable sum of money
from the revenues of the lease which he held with his

---

[1] Village in the district of Dolina, in the southern part of Eastern Galicia.

partners. The latter had then, after his disappearence, to pay the 80 ducats for the house which he had purchased. I saw with my own eyes the document, bearing the signature of Zaremba,[1] the treasurer of the landlord (of Bolechow), which showed that they had paid for the house.

Now I think it right to say something about the affairs of R. Abraham, son of R. Michel, some years previous to these last events. After the fire which occured at Bolechow in 519 (1759),[2] R. Abraham betook himself to Stanislawow,[3] and there entered into negotiations with Countess Kossakowska,[4] the owner of the salt-springs at Lisowice,[5] promising her a larger income from the springs. The Countess signified her assent to this proposal by a nod. On his way through Kalusz, R. Abraham talked to the Rabbi Zebi Hirsch, the son-in-law of the *Kazin* R. Joseph, who was afterwards appointed to be Rabbi here at Bolechow, and who in his last years held the position of Rabbi of Lemberg and its provinces.[6] R. Abraham boasted to the Rabbi how he had persuaded the Countess, the owner of the salt-springs at Lisowice, to give him the lease on condition that he guaranted to pay a higher rent (than that paid by the then leaseholder). The Rabbi, hearing all this, realised that R. Abraham was not fitted by his character and manners to judge the people of Israel. Accordingly he went himself with a party of his friends to Stanislawow, spoke with the Countess, and obtained from her the lease of the salt-springs without the knowledge of R. Abraham.

---

[1] A famous Polish noble family.

[2] See p. 101.

[3] Large commercial town in Eastern Galicia.

[4] Catherine Kossakowska, born Potocka, a lady well-known in the social life of the eighteenth century, was at that time owner of the estate of Stanislawow, which she acquired in 1771.

[5] Village in the district of Dolina, known up to 1826 for its salt-springs.

[6] R. Zebi Hirsch, son of R. Dob Ber. See S. Buber, *Anshé Shem* (Biographies of Lemberg rabbis), p. 197.

Then the "measure of the iniquities"[1] of R. Naḥman, the former holder of the lease of these salt-springs, was full. He had acquired this lease through fraud; at first he made an agreement with the brothers R. Joseph and R. Fischel of Stryi, who had previously held the lease, but afterwards he broke the agreement, and incited Gentiles to steal the horses of his partners, while he himself got up early in the morning and rode away to the proprietress and leased the salt-springs before the others could arrive. Although R. Naḥman became rich and well-known, his wealth was a stumbling-block and a source of grief to our community. In the first place, when the Elders of the Council of Four Lands met to appoint taxing officials to assess the Crown taxes to be paid by each community, the town of Bolechow was assessed as a place where wealthy people lived, because they said: "There is among you R. Naḥman, who could himself pay the whole of the sum imposed on you." Again, the fire and the looting committed on our community by the bandits in 519 (1759) were certainly due to the fame of the wealth of R. Naḥman. A year before the fire took place several peasants of Lisowice passed with their carts, drawn by oxen, through the vast forest on the side of the township of Solotwina, to the saltspring of Rosolna.[2] They there met bandits armed with fire-arms and axes, and said to them: "If you come to us you will find a Jew, the lease-holder of the salt-springs, who could fill all your sacks with golden ducats. But he keeps his money in a dome-shaped stone building which he owns at Bolechow." The following year the bandits made up their minds to invade the town of Dolina, but there was a guard of thirty men armed with fire-arms or carbines, and in addition all the inhabitants were keeping guard the whole night. The band was therefore afraid to raid Dolina, and marched the whole night and came at

---

[1] Sotah 9a.

[2] Both the township of Solotwina and the village of Rosolna are situated in the district of Bohorodczany, in Eastern Galicia.

dawn to Bolechow, as I have narrated on p...[1] All this came about as a result of the riches of the late R. Naḥman.

In that year — 525 (1765) — I ordered from the silver-smiths and goldsmiths at Lemberg, who were renowned for their skilful craftsmanship,[2] some sacred vessels made of pure silver for a Scroll of the Law belonging to R. Ensil Kaz of Tarczal. I ordered a large breastplate for the Scroll, made of solid silver, marked 14, beautifully ornamented, well plated with gold and set with precious stones, worth 80 Hungarian gulden; further, two silver rollers, nicely chased and also plated with gold, valued at 50 ducats; also a silvern pointer, very finely worked, worth 12 ducats. Many experts agreed that their like was not to be found throughout all Poland. The aged R. Leibush Malish,[3] a learned and famous Jewish leader, when he saw these ornaments together with the other Elders of the community, remarked: "Even in the time of King Solomon, peace be with him, these ornaments would have been fit for the Temple." He was at that time a great expert in all crafts.

In the month of Marḥesvan, 526 (16th October — 14th November 1765) I arrived at Tarczal and handed to R. Ensil Kaz all these sacred vessels. He was very pleased when he saw them and paid all the expenses I had incurred in obtaining them. He desired to present me with a cask of wine for my trouble, but I said: "I do not wish for any reward for the trouble I have taken in honour of the Torah."

I then bought 100 casks of wine from the wine-vaults of Queen Maria Teresa, and also I concluded a piece of business with a Greek merchant at Tarczal, who had his office in a shop on the main street of the town, over which he lived. Besides this I made some other purchases. Generally speaking, all the wines I got there were of good quality. But it was impossible to carry

---

[1] See p. 96 sq.
[2] See Introduction, p. 33.
[3] Apparently the one mentioned in S. Buber's Anshé Shem, p. 131, N. 341.

them to Lemberg before the fairs. I had to hire waggoners
to bring the wines away from Tarczal — they were
Swabians from the village of Rakamaz, which was situated on the other side of the river Theiss, opposite the
town of Tokay — and they brought the wines to the
village of Naman on the banks of the Theiss, but it was
impossible to drive the waggons through the river, because
it was all ice and snow, and a vessel was ice-bound on the
opposite shore. The Swabians, therefore, had to unload the
casks from the waggons and to put them in the field near
the bank of the river. They said that it might perhaps be
possible after a day or two to order drivers from the other
side of the river, who would take up the wines and carry
them across.

I was very angry with these Swabians, who had thrown
the casks from the waggons and left them lying all over
the field. I accordingly sent for the Elders of the village
of Naman; they came, and I complained to them that
the drivers had done me a great wrong, and that my
wines were now lying scattered over the field. I asked
the Elders to inquire if the casks were full, for I knew
that once when we spent the night where there was no
water for drinking the drivers might have opened one of
the casks. The peasants of the village brought instruments
and opened all the casks; we found that many of the casks
were short, and estimated that the deficiency altogether
amounted in value to 72 Rhenish gulden at least. This
amount was then deducted from the pay of the Swabians,
who returned to their homes.

The peasants of the village of Naman came along with
their sledges and loaded them with the wines after the
casks had been refilled and sealed by me, and stored them
in their homes until the river was completely frozen. I
spent nine days in that village and stayed with an old
Gentile of eighty years. The custom of this house was
that a fire should burn in the hearth all day, even if nothing was being cooked. Every member of the family
brought a little grid with a piece of bacon, roasted the

bacon at the fire and ate it. All night long this aged man
sat near the hearth, and slept sitting near the fire, which
was burning the whole time. He had wood prepared, which
was put on at intervals during the whole night, and thus
he did not allow the fire to go out.

What I saw there reminds me of what I have read about
fireworshippers. They are also mentioned in a passage
of the Talmud, which refers to the belief in two spirits,
the spirit of light and the spirit of darkness. The Hungarian people originated from those believers in the two
spirits.[1] The countries whence the Hungarians came
are situated near Media and Persia, where this religion
has ever since been established. Its founder was Gehazi,
the servant and pupil of the prophet Elisha, who was
driven away from his master for having accepted a present
from Naaman, the captain of the host of the King of Syria,
when he was cured from leprosy by the prophet Elisha,
as is explained in the second book of Kings, chapter 5,
verse 24. Driven away from his master, Gehazi betook
himself to a place where no one knew him. I have copied
from the books of the Gentiles all that Gehazi did in
establishing this religion, what faith he found existing
among the people, and what they learned from him. After
this creed had spread the Greeks called its followers
"magi." The Hungarians call themselves *"Magyar."* It
must, therefore, be that the Hungarian people came from
the countries in which this creed is practised. As I saw
in the house of the Hungarian that the fire never went
out, it must be that Gehazi had laid down that there
must always be a fire burning. The Greeks called Gehazi
Zoroaster.[2]

[1] Or principles, representing good and evil, or Ormuzd and Ahriman.

[2] On the fire-cult among the Hungarian people see Alexander Kovats, *De
antiqua gentili religione Hungariorum*, in *Compte rendu du quatrième Con-
grès scientifique international des Catholiques à Fribourg (Suisse) du 16 au
20 août 1897*, Fribourg, 1898, pp. 78—105. This survey of the old pagan
religion of the Hungarians deals also with various statements on the fire-
cult, which has survived in Hungary. Ber's narrative thus appears to be

Most of all I found (on this subject) in the work of
the author Humphrey Prideaux, an Englishman from the
town of London, who dealt at length with Gehazi in the
first part of his book.[1] Prideaux wrote also a full history
of all the nations who lived on the borders of the land
of Israel; he showed how all that the prophets had pre-
dicted concerning every nation and country was realized
and fulfilled. I have translated much of this book into
our holy Hebrew tongue. If God grants me that these
writings be printed, they will assuredly be a source of
great enlightenment to all our Jewish scholars. I do,
in particular, assure my sons and my descendants that
if they will apply themselves with diligence to read these
two books by the Englishman Humphrey — both the
German edition[2] and the Hebrew translation I have made
on the sheets of these books — they will assuredly acquire
from them great knowledge. This Humphrey knew not
only the Holy Bible, but also many subjects of the world's
history unknown to the Jewish people. We Jews must
know all things, so that there may be realised in us the
saying from the Bible: "For this is your wisdom and your

a corroboration of the fact that the fire-cult had a strong tradition in that
country. His attempt to connect the Hungarians with the creed of Zoroaster
is, of course, merely curious, but it illustrates his liking for historical research.

[1] *The Old and New Testament connected in the History of the Jews and
the neighbouring Nations from the Declension of the Kingdoms of Israel
and Judah to the time of Christ*, London, 1716—18. Ber refers to vol. I,
Book III, p. 179 and Book IV, p. 211. Prideaux does not say (as might be
assumed from what Ber writes) that Gehazi was the founder of Parseeism;
he simply mentions, in referring to different opinions as to the origin of
Zoroaster, that some have identified him with Gehazi. Again, the details
of Ber's story of the migration of Gehazi to a far country are not to be
found in Prideaux's account. Ber must have had some other source or
sources.

[2] *Alt und Neu Testament in eine Connexion mit der Juden und benach-
barten Voelker Historie gebracht vom Verfall der Reiche Israel und Juda
an bis auf Christi Himmelfahrt.* The author of this translation, the first
edition of which was published in Dresden, in 1726, was D. Valentin Ernst
Loescher. — Ber relates further on how this German translation of Prideaux's
work reached him.

understanding in the sight of the nations."[1] Although our
teachers, be their memories for a blessing, applied this
saying to our holy *Torah*, they also taught that it is good
to combine the *Torah* with wordly knowledge; and it is
advantageous for every intelligent and educated Jew to
have a knowledge of the history of the nations of the
world. This will sometimes enable him properly to answer
questions directed against the Jewish Law and faith, as
has occurred to me several times in my discourses with
the nobles and the clergy. In most of the cases I have
found the right answer, and it is well-known to all that
my replies were always convincing. But let us return to
our business affairs.

I arrived at Lemberg with the wines and sold them
at a good price. Every day more and more false silver
coins appeared, and the ducats increased in value until
they were changed at 27 gulden each.[2] The sale of the
wines proceeded fairly well — no one cask having been
sold for less than 17 or 18 ducats — but the loss on the
exchange out-weighed the profit. We therefore did not
trouble to collect our debts for our wines from the nobles,
our customers, and those noblemen who had lent us
money also did not care to collect the sums we owed
them, for they had learned that a new value for the
gulden was about to be fixed, which actually meant
a new reduction in the standard of the coinage.[3] This
happened in the following year, as I will explain in
its place and in its time, in accordance with the truth,
if God will.

Now I will tell of the great change brought about in
the Polish country with the purpose of humiliating our
people of Israel, and of the taking away of that little
honour they had always enjoyed since the time they came

[1] Deut. 4 [6].

[2] See Introduction, p. 27.

[3] Ber refers to reductions which had taken place in 1761 and 1762. The
whole question of the devaluation of Polish money in the sixties of the
eighteenth century is dealt with in the Introduction, p. 27—28.

to settle in Poland, 900 years ago,[1] until King Poniatowski ascended the throne. In those days the Polish
nobles asserted that the Elders of the Council of Four
Lands, the Chiefs of Israel, who had always to meet at
Warsaw during the sessions of the Diet in connection
with the poll-taxes to be paid by the Jews to the Crown,
caused the dissolution of the Diets, which had been convoked at great expense. Every Diet was attended by
many deputies, Jew-baiters, who denounced the Jews for
every kind of wickedness, in order to deprive them of the
liberties they had always enjoyed, and proposed to forbid
the Jews to carry on profitable businesses in wine, cattle
and other goods. Under the constitution of Poland one
member of the Diet, i. e. "*Szlachticz*" (noble), could stop
the business of the session by declaring: "I do not agree to
this matter."[2] The Polish nobles believed that the leading
Jews bribed some of the deputies to bring the sessions
of the Diets to an end by this means. The Government
therefore decreed that the Jewish Council should be abolished, that non-Jewish comissioners should be sent throughout Poland to number the Jewish population, and that the
Jews should pay taxes according to their numbering, and
thus all the rights of our Assemblies would be abrogated.
At the same time the Government, by consent of all the
noblemen, the deputies of the Great Diet at Warsaw,
decided to annul the compact which had always existed
between the Elders of Four Lands, on the one hand, and
the State Treasurer, on the other, concerning the governmental poll-tax. Under this compact the Jews had to pay
yearly to the State Treasurer 3oo,ooo gulden. The Elders
of Four Lands convoked deputies elected in all the communities of the four Polish provinces,[3] and from among

---

[1] This statement is somewhat vague. The first appearance of the Jews
in Poland does not go back beyond the eleventh century; and these early
traces of a Jewish settlement in that country have not yet been established.

[2] The notorious "Liberum veto." See Introduction, p. 19.

[3] Great Poland, Little Poland, Red Russia (District of Lemberg) and
Volhynia.

those deputies were appointed wise men who knew how
to estimate the capacity of every community. to pay taxes.
Great Rabbis also conferred with them in order to draw
up proper regulations in accordance with the Jewish law,
so that the Jews need not come before the non-Jewish
High Courts. These Rabbis laid down regulations, in
accordance with our holy *Torah*, to cover whatever was
not explained in the books of our ancient teachers; and
these regulations were accepted by the communities like
the *Torah*, and were called "The Books of Regulations
of the Four Lands."[1] I saw these books printed when I
was still a child. The Rabbis met continually side by side
with the Elders of the Four Lands. Every important legal
affair which occurred in the communities of Poland was
brought before this High Court of Rabbis. This wise
institution among the Jewish communities lasted for 800
years and more.[2] It was a small solace and a little honour
too, proving that Almighty God in his great pity and
great loving-kindness had not deserted us; as it is said in
the *Torah* of Moses "And yet for all that, when they be in
the land of their enemies, I will not cast them away, neither
will I abhor them; for I am the Lord their God."[3] But,
on account of our many sins, when the new King, Poniatowski, ascended the throne of Poland and was crowned,
in 1764, he at once ordered, in agreement with the Great

---

[1] These "Books" are no longer preserved. We know of various decisions
of these Jewish Councils published in many rabbinical works (see Lewin's
lists of these works in his *Neue Materialien zur Geschichte der Vierländer-
synode*, I and III). We know also of some sheets belonging to the original
minutes of the Council of Four Lands, but we do not possess the "Books"
of which Ber speaks here.

[2] This statement is not correct. The Jewish Assemblies came into existence in the first half of the sixteenth century. See S. Dubnow, *Council
of Four Lands*, in *Jew. Enc.*, vol. IV; idem. *The History of the Jews in
Russia and Poland*, Philadelphia, 1916, vol. I, pp. 188 et *seq.*; M. Balaban,
The Central Organ of Jewish Self Government in Poland in *The History
of the Jewish People*, (R.), Moscow, 1914, vol. XI; M. Lewin, *Neue Materialien*, etc. III, 1916, pp. 38—40.

[3] Lev. 26[44].

Diet (called the Convocation Diet, because all the nobles were then present at Warsaw),[1] the counting of the Jews by non-Jewish commissioners, in all the provinces of Poland. He also ordained that every Jew should pay two gulden every year in two instalments, one in March, or *Adar*, and the other in August, or *Elul*.

When the commissioners arrived at our place — the chief of the commission being a certain Gromnicki, whom I knew well — I took it upon myself to advise the servants of the community to tell everybody to conceal the number of their children as much as possible. I similarly advised the Elders of the community, assuring them that no harm would come to our people, even if they should conceal the numbers of all our poor. My advice was followed. There were then in our community more than 1300 people, but the number given to the commissioners, and entered in their books, as the Jewish population of Bolechow and the surrounding villages was 883. But the commissioners said: "According to our instructions from the capital, Warsaw, two Elders of the community must take an oath that you have given us the real number." We had therefore to send two Elders, the Rabbi of the community of Busk, R. Hirschel,[2] and R. Solomon, son of R. Gerson, an old and respected man. They went to the town of Zydaczow and there they took the oath.

---

[1] Convocation Diet was the name given to the Diet summoned after the death of a King to convoke the Election Diet. The Convocation Diet to which Ber alludes was held in May and June, 1764. The question how to increase the revenues from the Jewish taxes occupied the members of the Diet at several sittings. See the official *Diary of the Convocation Diet at Warsaw Which Lasted Seven Weeks*, etc. (1764), Warsaw (P.). — The Jewish Councils or Assemblies were abolished by a resolution of the General Confederation, which was convened by the Czartoryscy in July, 1764. See *Volumina legum*, vol. VII, p. 167. Our author is therefore inaccurate in saying that King Stanislaus Augustus was already crowned when this happened. The Election Diet only met on the 16th August, and was closed on the 26th after Stanislaus Augustus had been elected. See R. Nisbet Bain, *The Last King of Poland*, pp. 66 and 70.

[2] See Buber, *Anshé Shem*, p. 248.

So the commissioners confirmed the number given by us, and put it in the official lists as the basis upon which the taxes were to be collected; and on that basis we paid six contributions during three years. To this day I have in my possession the receipts printed in Polish, which show that we paid one contribution every half year.

The Elders of the Council of Four Lands, the Rabbis and other prominent and leading Jews appeared before the Government and the nobles, the deputies of the Diet, with a great petition, asking that justice might be done to them. They represented that they had incurred heavy debts because of the great expenses caused by their journeys to the sessions of the Council of Four Lands, and also to the sessions of the Diet at Warsaw, and did not know how to meet them. This petition was favourably received by the Government and the nobles, the deputies of the Diet. A decree was passed unanimously to collect from the Jews three levies, that is, three gulden annually in order to pay all the debts and claims of the Jewish Elders. Commissioners were sent forthwith to Lemberg to transmit this decree to the various districts, ordering that the poll-tax (from the Jews) should be collected in three levies, and strict orders were given to the landlords of the towns in which Jewish settlements existed to compel the Jews to hasten the payment of this poll-tax. The Jewish communities had to obey this command, and they collected from their people the money that was to be paid, relentlessly and without remorse,[1] in order to avoid the still further expenses that would have arisen as a result of collection by distraint. The members of our community at Bolechow sent me the sum due from them in silver gulden. This coin was then worth 15 Polish *grosz*, that is, $7^{1}/_{2}$ *kreuzcr* of Imperial (Austrian) money.[2]

[1] Dr. M. Lewin in his *Neue Materialien*, etc., 1916, p. 14, annotation 61, misinterprets this passage to mean that the Jews had to pay three levies for the expenses of the Elders, and two levies for the poll-tax. In fact, as stated on the previous page, they had to pay three gulden instead of two. See Introduction, p. 37.

[2] Before the devaluation 15 or 19 kreuzer. See Introduction, p. 27.

The Jewish Elders hastened to meet in Lemberg with
the object of collecting the outstanding debts. Many
of them knew and esteemed my brother, the learned
R. Aryeh Loeb, who had been many a time representative
of our community at various meetings. At a meeting held
at Bobrka[1] he had been unanimously elected an Elder of
the Council of Four Lands, and his name was inscribed in
the minutes of that Council. When they now met for the
last time at Lemberg, many of the Elders stayed in houses
which were near by and visible to us. Those present at
the Assembly[2] included the representatives of Brody, viz.
the learned Elder R. Leibush, son-in-law of the *Parnas*[3]
of the Four Lands, R. Berush; R. Leibush, son of this
R. Berush, Rabbi of Zbaraz and later appointed Chief
Rabbi over all the communities in Galicia;[4] R. Hirsch,
another son of R. Berush, Rabbi at the Tailors' Synagogue
in Brody.[5] Besides these three there were some other representatives of Brody and of other communities. The
community of Tysmienica delegated R. Siskind, son of
R. Kalman, and other deputies. The community of Zolkiew[6] was also represented there, and there were present

[1] A place south-East of Lemberg, at which several meetings of representatives of Jewish communities of the district of Red Ruthenia were held.
See Dr. I. Schipper, *Beiträge zur Geschichte der partiellen Judentage in
Polen um die Wende des XVII. und XVIII. Jahrhunderts bis zur Auflösung
des jüdischen Parlamentarismus*, in *Monatsschrift für Geschichte und Wisssen-
schaft des Judentums*, 1912.

[2] Here Ber uses the term *Vaad*, that is Assembly, which conveys a clearer
idea of that peculiar organ of Jewish self-government than the word "Council".
See Introduction, p. 38.

[3] Elder.

[4] His epitaph has been recently published by Dr. N. M. Gelber, *Aus dem
Pinax des alten Judenfriedhofs in Brody*, in *Jahrbuch der Jüdisch-Literari-
schen Gesellschaft*, Frankfurt (on the Main), vol. XIII, 1920, p. 134. The
same author deals with the activities of R. Leibush in his capacity as Chief
Rabbi in Galicia, in the Russian-Jewish historical quaterly *Yevreyskaia
Starina*, 1914, Petrograd, pp. 305—317.

[5] His epitaph is in the article of Dr. N. M. Gelber quoted above,
p. 134.

[6] North of Lemberg.

in addition the Rabbi of Swierz[1] and other deputies with him. They came early in the morning to our house to talk to my brother and consult him with regard to the affairs of the Council of Four Lands. They asked for his advice as to how to speak to the nobles and how to obtain what they desired. Now the fruit of the vine was never lacking in our house; everybody has need of him who has wine; and as our sages, be their memories for a blessing, said in their time: "When the wine comes in, the secret comes out."[2] So I gathered from the conversation of the Elders that the amount collected from the poll-tax paid by the people exceeded by a good deal the amount of the debts incurred by the Elders of the Council of Four Lands; and I thought that perhaps it would be a good thing if I did not pay the contribution of our community, but allowed the money to remain in our hands. Fearing, however, lest our community should be punished for not having sent the quota due from them in accordance with the decree of the crown, I used every now and then to send to the cashier one of our clerks, who, when he saw that the cashier was very busy paying or receiving money, would approach him and say: "Sir, I have brought the money from the community of Bolechow." Whereupon the cashier would reply: "Do you not see that I have not a minute free? Come another time." We did this many times, until the office was closed. Then, after the debts of the Chiefs and Rabbis of the Four Lands were repaid, I went myself to the cashier Zaremba, who knew me well, as his brother was Marshal of the Court of our landlord, and said to him: "Why did you refuse to take the money from the community of Bolechow? I sent it several times, but it was not accepted." He replied: "What could I do? Your clerks saw that I was busy." "Then," said I, "I would ask my lord to acknowledge by certificate that I brought the

---

[1] Township south-east of Lemberg.

[2] Erubin 65 a. *Cf.* the English saying: "When the wine is in, the wit is out."

money, but that it was impossible for him to accept it
owing to pressure of work, as my lord had to receive
many sums from a large number of Jewish communities,
and had himself to distribute the money and pay to each
of the Elders the amount due to him." He wrote the
certificate (I asked for) with his own hand and sealed it
with his seal; (it was stated therein) that I had brought
the money due from the community of Bolechow, but he
could not accept it for the reason just explained. He
sealed this certificate in due form, like a receipt for money.
Then I immediately returned all the money to our community by a special messenger, my brother, the learned
R. Seeb Wolf, who was at that time returning home on
our horse; he carried the heavy packet to Bolechow, and
handed it over, sealed as it was, to the Chiefs of the
community. The horse's back was seriously injured by
the weight of the silver money he had to carry. This
horse was then worth more than 10 ducats, but his injury
made him unfit for any more work. Nevertheless, the
Elders of the community at Bolechow did not recognise
the kindness I had showed them in saving such a large
sum of money, as it were from the lion's mouth. Some
of the leaders of the community wanted to quarrel with
me because of the hate engendered in their hearts by
the envy they bore me, which grew greater than ever
now that I had done so great a service to the whole of
our congregation. But whatever they devised to hurt
me, the Lord in His compassion will turn to my benefit.
There is no need to speak further of human foolishness.

After the Elders and Chiefs of the Council of Four
Lands had been removed from their little position of
importance, and after this small honour had been taken
away from Israel, the words of the prophet were fulfilled:
"For Israel has not been forsaken, nor Judah of his God,
of the Lord of Hosts."[1] In that, or the following year,
that is in 527 (1767), the prophecy of Ezekiel, contained in

[1] Jer. 51⁵.

chapter 25, verse 14, was fulfilled: "And I will lay my
vengeance upon Edom by the hand of my people Israel."
For in that year began the Confederation, that is, a revolt
against the Crown and the Senate in Warsaw.[1] The majority of the nobles said one to another: "The Polish
people has been free from time immemorial. We have
no dealings with Poniatowski, nor any counsel with his
Senate at Warsaw."[2] So the powerful nobles made a
great conspiracy and concluded a strong covenant. They
raised large sums of money among themselves, and, as
they acted on the advice of France, 200,000 ducats were
sent to them from Paris.[3] I saw this with my own eyes,
for the officer who brought the money stayed with me a
whole day. The turmoil lasted for five years throughout
the whole of Poland. During that time there was no
law nor justice in the country, but "might was right."[4]
The nobles called that period Pod Kaptur;[5] it ended when
the whole State was divided, in 1772. Then the Polish
people and their kingdom were deprived of all honour,
and the verse was fulfilled: "And I will lay my vengeance
upon Edom" — that is, the Polish nation, Gentiles being
called Edom — "by the hand of my people Israel" — that
is to say, that as they had dealt with Israel, so were they
dealt with. All the honour of their country was taken
away from them, and they were enslaved for ever. And
so perish our foes who denounce us! This is enough for
those who understand and know the history of our fore-
fathers. If the Almighty decrees for me further years of

[1] The Confederation of Bar began on 29th February, 1768, and lasted
for five years.
[2] II. Sam. 20[1] and 16[28].
[3] Rulhiere, Histoire de l'anarchie de Pologne et du demembrement
de cette république, Paris, 1807, vol. IV, p. 101, states that France agreed
to send 6,000 ducats monthly. See also H. Schmitt, Polish History in the
18th and 19th centuries, 1866 (P.), p. 298.
[4] Sotah, 60b.
[5] During an interregnum, when the ordinary Law Courts suspended their
activities, extraordinary Courts called Kaptur Courts were installed.

life, I will tell you more of the experiences of our fore-
fathers, the sons of Israel, in their bitter dispersion, by
the compassion of God. But we will now return to our
commercial affairs.

At that time the value of the gulden was very poor,
the silver contained in it being worth 5 *kreuzer* of Imperial
(Austrian) money. It was very difficult for Polish merchants to go to foreign countries for the purpose of trade,
because ducats were expensive — up to 27 gulden. My
brother, R. Aryeh Loeb, went to Brody to exchange
ducats there, and R. Leibush, the rabbi of Zbaraz,[1] with
whom he stayed, lent him 3,000 gulden. When my brother
returned from Brody, I travelled to Hungary. I stopped
at Tarczal, where I bought from the nobleman Patay
50 casks of wine at 5 ducats per cask. At Mad I bought
from the nobleman Szepeszi 60 casks of *máslás* of a fine
aroma at 6 ducats per cask. I also bought 15 casks at
Tarczal from R. Judah Loeb, and paid for them 160 ducats. Besides these and other purchases made for our
firm, I bought 16 casks of wine for the noble Mrozowicki,
the Starosta of Stengwil,[2] who had given to me 150 ducats
before I left for Hungary. I carried these 16 casks of
wine to the village of Sokoliwka, near the township of
Bobrka. We made an account of the expenses involved
in the purchase, and, adding to these expenses some previous debts, Mrozowicki remained indebted to us for a
sum of 58 ducats. In that year, however, the Confederation
began, and Mrozowicki, together with our landlord, the
Cup-Bearer Potocki, went out to fight the Muscovite army
of 24,000 which the king of Poland had put in the field
against the revolting nobles.[3] This war lasted for five
years, and Mrozowicki did not repay his debt until he
returned home.

[1] See p. 147.

[2] Adam Mrozowicki; see Niesiecki, *Polish Heraldry* (P.).

[3] Whilst the Confederation of Bar was supported by France, King Stanislaus Augustus Poniatowski had to invite the Russians to march against the
troops of the Confederation.

The wines I had purchased in Hungary I brought to Lemberg, but there was no possibility of selling them, because the silver in the false coins grew less and less, and the merchants had to offer their goods on credit to their customers. Hungarian wines in particular, which the nobles used to buy, could not be sold to them otherwise than on credit, and it was impossible to get any money from them even at the expiration of the term of the credit, as silver became more and more rare. In the meantime the season approached when we had to leave for Hungary, but we had not ready money enough to meet our obligations there, although we enjoyed great credit with the nobles, and with Jews and Gentiles generally. Our acquaintances and friends were very eager to assist us with a loan, most of all the superintendent of all the Custom Houses of Poland, Skirmunt, who was willing to lend us several hundred ducats; but he was unable to collect any money from his debtors. He kept us at Lemberg for weeks, sending out letters, written in our presence, in which he requested his debtors to lend him at least some money, but they all excused themselves on the ground that they had none.

We then approached our landlord, the Cup-Bearer of the Crown,[1] who was passing through Lemberg at that time. After listening to us he replied: "I will give you some good advice. Do not keep your wines at Lemberg henceforth, for I shall be unable to protect them from robbery and pillage, which may take place here in Lemberg in future. It would be better for you to store your wines in your own home at Bolechow." From this I understood that the war I referred to above was about to break out. So we went to our home, and took with us the wines we had left at Skole. We did not attend any more fairs of Lemberg, for we could not ignore the warning of our landlord not to take much wine thither. Our noble creditors were very astonished at our delay

[1] Above Ber refers to him correctly as the Cup-Bearer of Lithuania.

in coming to the fairs; most of them, however, relied upon
our honesty, knowing that in time we would meet our
obligations. None of them came to our home to demand
payment except a certain Gorzewski, then the landlord of
the township of Kalendsan,[1] in the vicinity of Kamieniec-
Podolsk, who came to collect the 3oo ducats we owed
him together with a year's interest. Some people of
our community, who had always hated and envied us,
were pleased at our difficulty. "Now," they said, "the day
which we have hoped for has arrived, the day which
will witness the downfall of the family of the Breser[2],
who have always prospered. If this noble takes from
them all their possessions, they will become as poor as
we." The wives and the children of our enemies also
rejoiced at our bad fortune. I myself saw a lady of one
of the prominent families pass by our house with her
daughter-in-law on purpose, as she said, "to see what
the noble is going to do to them;" for she had never
before passed that way. Besides this we heard other
insults from people who hated us out of pure envy and
none of whom we had ever harmed. On the contrary,
there was not one who had not received a favour from
us, particularly from my revered brother, R. Aryeh Loeb,
who had always stood up for his people and defended
the interests of the whole community, as I have partly
related above.

Nevertheless, the compassion of Heaven did not fail us.
God softened the heart of this noble, so that he agreed
to accept from us one of the promissory notes which we
held from other nobles for their debts to us, and we
gave him the promissory note of Morawski, the brother-

---

[1] Apparently a misscript. This name does not occur in the classical
Polish *Geographical Dictionary*, which contains a full description of even
the smallest villages of Poland.

[2] Ber assumed in the Austrian time — Bolechow became Austrian in
1772 together with Galicia — the surname of Birkenfeld. Breser or Brzesier
is derived from the Polish *brzoza*, the German *Birke*. This is the only
place in the Memoirs where the family surname occurs.

in-law of the renowned Prince Radziwil.[1] Our creditor
Gorzewski gave us a receipt for our debt on condition
that if Morawski paid the 7000 gulden he owed us, then
our debt to him would be wiped out. He then left for
Lemberg, and we remained in suspense, knowing that
if he did not receive the money there he could claim it
from us. When he arrived at Lemberg Gorzewski learned
that another nobleman, named Czaikowski, had demanded
from Morawski payment of 2,000 gulden on a promissory
note bearing our signatures, and, furthermore, produced
a letter of transfer[2] issued by us, which said that we had
sold to Czaikowski the right to receive from Morawski
2,000 gulden out of the sum of 7,000 gulden he owed us.
This letter produced by Czaikowski was forged; for he
had taken leave of his senses, and had written this document himself, and paid a Jew at Lemberg, to whom he
showed our signatures on the promissory note, to forge
them on the letter of transfer. When Gorzewski saw this,
he was very angry, for, although it was clear that Czaikowski had forged the letter of transfer, Gorzewski considered it humiliating to come as an agent of ours to
demand our debt on our authorisation, and not by a
deed of transfer like that produced by the other noble.
Accordingly Gorzewski had to send to us a clever Polish
lawyer with a letter in which he asked us to give him
a letter of transfer for the whole of the debt of Morawski,
so that it should be his absolute property, and he should
not appear simply as our agent. I then had to go to
Zydaczow, the seat of the Court of the Starosta,[3] where
I handed the lawyer the documents of Morawski, and he
declared us free of our debt of 300 ducats to Gorzewski.
This is stated in the rolls of the Court of Zydaczow.
Then also the debt of 2,000 gulden, which Czaikowski

---

[1] Ignatius Morawski, Marshal of the High Court of Lithuania, married
in 1765 the Princess Teofila Radziwil. See Niesiecki, *Polish Heraldry* (P.).

[2] In Polish *cesya*.

[3] Zydaczow, town south-east of Lemberg.

demanded from us, was declared null and void. I have
to this day an envelope full of documents, sealed with
the seal of the Court of Lemberg, where it is shown that
this debt has been declared null and void.

Now I will tell, by the way, of a great wonder the
Almighty did for us in connection with a Gentile who
had a promissory note of ours for the sum of 5,318
gulden, besides interest on it for some eight years. This
man was named Abramowski, and was a native of Lithuania. When he was in Brody during the first great fire
there, in 1742,[1] he managed to obtain some spoiled goods,
and left the town with great riches. Since then this
Abramowski has been engaged in lending money on mortgage. When the nobles were in need he lent them what
they wanted on the security of villages which he held
and had cultivated by the help of the serfs living in them.
He made large profit by the sale of the grain, and thus
amassed great wealth. In his old age he came to Lemberg, and having always been friendly with us, and
knowing us for good people, stayed in our home and
lived with us some months during the summer. Later
on he moved from Lemberg and settled in a village
near the township of Mosciska.[2] During the Fairs he
always used to come to Lemberg, but he could not find
us there.[3]

After the partition of Poland, when the Imperial Law
Courts had been established, this Abramowski appeared
before the Judge of Mosciska and produced a promissory
note of ours, requesting the Judge to exact from us his
debt, which ran to 5,318 gulden besides interest for
over six years.[4] During the Fairs of that year I met
Abramowski, blind in both eyes, and a little Gentile boy
was leading him. I then went and talked about him with

[1] See p. 85.
[2] West of Lemberg.
[3] See p. 152, where Ber relates that he and his brother did not attend the
Fairs during the years of anarchy.
[4] Just before Ber had written "eight years."

R. Tobia Komarner, an honest man, in whose house he was staying; and R. Tobia told me how Abramowski had handed over the promissory note to the judge, as related above. On hearing this I raised my eyes to Heaven and said: "The Almighty who has helped me till now will help me again and for ever." I then went to speak to Abramowski, who was very glad when he heard my voice, and asked after the health of my wife and children. I answered him: "All is well, only it is impossible for us to get our many debts settled by the nobles in a legal way. They are not willing to pay anything for the good wines they took from us for their needs; and some are not in a position to pay their debts. For this reason we also cannot settle our many obligations, though we have always been accustomed to pay at the fixed time, as you know, Sir. You will, Sir, forgive me the delay in paying our debt. We are not doing it with any dishonest intent. The hard and grievous times have compelled many respected and well-known merchants to leave their business and to lose their property, even Gentile business-people, and what can we do, we unhappy Jews? The Almighty knows the uprightness of our hearts." Abramowski was greatly moved, tears streamed down his cheeks, and he said: "It is true. I have always known the honesty of your heart, which has ever been well disposed towards all mankind. May heaven pity you." I then asked: "Why do you want, Sir, to begin an endless law-suit with us? Who would be acquitted by the law, and who could bear the heavy expenses of the case?" I used other persuasive arguments, and R. Tobia also strongly advocated our cause, while his wife particularly was very eloquent, until Abramowski agreed to return to us the promissory note without any payment, except some ducats for his expenses. We agreed to pay him 12 ducats for his personal expenses, besides a barrel of wine. Our promissory note was, however, not with Abramowski, as he had already handed it to the Judge of Mosciska. Abramowski, therefore, went with me to the office of the Court of the *Voyevoda*[1] and asked the clerk, Rogalski, to make out a receipt freeing me of all liabilities towards him. He signed himself the records of the Court, and the receipt was duly made out for 5,318 Polish gulden, with accrued interest for so many years. Thus was God's grace manifestly granted me, in that I was saved from such a great obligation. At that time there was staying in the inn of R. Tobia, where Abramowski lived, the learned R. Isaac Hindes; he saw what the Lord had done for me, and was greatly astonished.

The winter I spent at home. The time was just approaching to farm out the revenues of the town, but no one of our community was inclined to take up the lease, as the former holders of it had lost much in this business owing to the practices of the steward, Bobrowski, whose object was to rob the Jews of their gains by violence. He, as already related above, had forced some of our people to go and settle in the new township of Podwysokie.[2] Other Jewish people had to take up the lease of the revenues of Bolechow in order to avoid being banished to the new place. In 527 (1767) the lease was held by the Elder of the community R. Simel; the learned R. Judah Loeb, son of R. Schneur; the learned R. David, son of R. Ber and grandson of R. David Kaz; and the Elder of the community R. Naphtali Herz, son of R. Joseph. It would serve no purpose to enumerate all the other partners in the enterprise, as, for instance, R. Loeb Nyniower and others; suffice it to say that all of them lost a considerable sum in paying the fee for the lease, which was over 18,000 ducats, each ducat then being worth 27 gulden.

At that time our landlord, the Cup-Bearer, began the rebellion against the Crown of Poland, as was related

---

[1] In Polish times the Courts where lawsuits between Jews and Gentiles were heard. This affair with Abramowski, however, took place under the Austrian régime. Ber uses the old term for a new Austrian office.

[2] See p. 133.

on page ... The steward, Bobrowski, refused to support him in this insurrection, and retired from his service. Our landlord spent the winter alone and in secret in his fine palace in the town of Trembowla,[1] writing letters day and night to the nobles of Poland, his friends and acquaintances, to be ready for a united uprising against the enemy, at the moment when the Confederation should be called together.[2] The revenues of the estates remained under the control of the stewards in each place. Every steward was trying to induce the Elders of the respective communities to help him to find a trustworthy person to take over the lease of the revenues of his town. Here at Bolechow no one wanted to hold the lease, being afraid of the losses involved. The Elders of our community and the steward, seeing that no one was willing to take the lease, cast their eyes on me, and attempted to persuade me to be the lease-holder. Besides these, our Rabbi, Hirsch, advised me to take up the lease, as it would be to my benefit. He argued that our creditors would be impressed by this honourable position of ours, and that our landlord would be obliged to protect us against them. The steward Majewski in particular promised to help me with all his power in the affairs of the lease during the whole year. He also made an allowance in the price, for a year before the price had been 18,000 gulden, but now the contract was concluded for a sum of 16,000 gulden. I consented the more readily to hold the lease, as my neighbours, R. Asriel Selig, son of R. Ber Menaker, R. Abra-

[1] In the south-eastern part of Galicia.

[2] Count Joachim Potocki, the Cup-Bearer of Lithuania, was among the most ardent promoters of the Confederation of Bar. Ber's evidence is here as in other cases of the highest interest. It is an important contribution to our knowledge of that episode in Polish history. In the *Memoirs* of the Polish poet, Francisk Karpinski, published in 1898, p. 38, reference is made to the "noisy universals" (appeals) with the watchword "faith and liberty", which were dispatched by the Confederates. Karpinski, then 26 years old, was staying with the noble Bielski at Pieniaki (in Galicia), when the Confederation of Bar began, in 1768.

ham, son of R. Seeb Wolf, and R. David, son of R. Samuel
Menaker, who formerly held the lease of the mills and
the tolls and were thus experienced in this kind of business, promised to support me in good faith and to assist
me in the affairs of the lease, so that all would be well.
These people pointed out to me that they knew the way
to make profit in this business, which they had practised
for many years. My friends said: "It is of no use for you
to engage clerks and servants at great expense for this
business; you had better give some share of the profits
which the Almighty will grant to your partners. They
will surely behave in this affair as if it were their own
business, and act honestly, not like officials, of whom
it was said 'the more men-servants, the more robbery'." [1]
So I took the lease in proper form. I ordered a cash-
box to be made, divided into six compartments, each of
which had a hole through which money could be put, so
that each of the various fees should go into its proper
compartment. Further, I prepared two account-books
made of two pounds of paper, one for the wine-shops
and the other for the mills. The registers were ruled on
each page. Every fee was to be entered on its page in
small writing, its source and the person by whom it was
paid. The sums of money were to be written in proper
order, every one in its own line. I thought that my partners would be pleased that I had introduced proper order
into the holding of the lease; and so they were, until a
person who hated me because of the envy he had always
borne me said to them: "Of what use is it to follow his
advice and to keep such registers, which no other Jew
uses in his business? He certainly intends to rob you of
all the fruits of your labour. You are working day after
day on the lease, whilst he sits at home and makes the
profit." By these and other slanders he turned my partners against me. As a matter of fact, during the first
week that I held the liquor-lease in my house all the

[1] *Ethics of the Fathers*, Chapter II.

Gentiles of our town and their wives and children came
in great glee, and consumed much liquor, for which they
paid in cash, to the amount of several hundred gulden.
But after my partners had talked with my enemy they
took the sale of liquor from me and transferred it to
the house of my neighbour, R. Baruch of Cerkowna, a
relative of theirs. The result was that during a whole
week only 17 gulden were received. The sales dwindled
more and more, and no money was seen; the liquor was
given to the Gentiles on credit. In the other branches of
the lease, the mills and the customs revenues, my partners
acted on their own initiative. After a quarter of a year
I looked into the accounts, the registers and the cash-box
of the lease, and there was a great shortage, so much so
that it was impossible to find cash for the payment of
half the amount due for the quarter. I was very upset
that I had been brought into such danger. This, I thought,
would bring me more harm than all the other misfortunes
which had so long dogged me. As regards the debts which
I had to repay the distant nobles I could always approach
our landlord to assist us in one way or another, either by
coming to an agreement with the creditors, or beginning
a law-suit before the Courts; but when it was a matter
of paying our landlord himself — how could we afford
to quarrel with someone who was more powerful than
we? I was very frightened and grieved. I raised my eyes
to Heaven, asking: "Whence will come my help?"

It happened just then that the marshal of the court
of our landlord, his highest official, Zaremba, arrived with
an order from our landlord for the dismissal of the steward
Maiewski, and the appointment in his stead of a certain
Dembowanz, who was instructed to look into the affairs
of the estate of Bolechow. The partners then said: "Perhaps we could ask this gentleman to agree to some new
regulations of the lease in order to improve the revenues?"
Acting on their suggestion, I composed a petition explain-
ining the wishes of the lease-holders. I then went to the
marshal, handed him the petition, and talked openly to him.

"How can our landlord," asked I, "expect me to lose on
his lease? I have never had experience in these matters.
I was never a lease-holder, and I never gained a farthing
from any lease in the world, as since my youth I have
always been a wine-trader. I was introduced into that
business by my parents, and for twenty-five years I have
carried on that occupation in Lemberg, as it is known to
everybody. Now I have left Lemberg and brought some
wines to Bolechow. I did it on the advice of our landlord,
be his lordship exalted, who advised us not to carry wines
to Lemberg, as in view of the robberies and pillage that
would take place there he would not be able to protect us;
so that it would be better to keep the wines in our homes
at Bolechow." Zaremba listened to my speech, and replied:
"You must go and order that the petition be written in
another manner, in accordance with your words." I took
back the paper I had brought and went to write another
petition, appealing to the landlord to consider if it were
right that I should lose. I pointed out that for more than
twenty years, since my youth, I had been engaged in a
reputable trade in far-off lands and in foreign places. Now,
when I had come to take refuge under the wings of his
lordship, I had agreed to farm his revenues, not in order
to make a profit, but to see that his revenues did not
decrease. Now, in consequence of bad times, it appeared
that there would be a great loss on the lease, which we
were not able to bear. What benefit would it bring to
the treasury of the landlord if I, a poor man, should be
utterly ruined, after I had left so much wine at Lemberg
for lost? I further explained that many nobles obtained
wine from us on credit for considerable amounts, but
that it now appeared impossible to get any money from
them. We had suffered heavy losses because of the
decline in the value of the gulden in recent years: everyone knew how the merchants had suffered from this
decline. How could our landlord not pity us, and allow
us to lose everything when we had always been his
devoted subjects?

Further, I composed a nicely worded petition in the name of the Elders of the Community, concerning the salary of the Rabbi. Our community had to pay to the treasury of the landlord 80 ducats yearly out of the revenue of the *Gabelle*, or slaughter-tax. I made it clear in this petition that the people of our community had always had worthy Rabbis, and that at that time we had a Rabbi of very high merit and renown; and he could not give us even the third part of the eighty ducats that we had to pay to the treasury.

Finally, I wrote a third petition in the name of the whole community concerning the duty from cochineal or crimson dye, which was required for the trade in woollen girdles. The tax on this trade had recently been farmed for 800 gulden; but as the trade was carried on by the poor people of our community, they petitioned the landlord to lighten the burden which fell on them by reason of this duty.

The landlord replied to us personally on all three petitions, thus showing us great kindness To the first petition he answered that he was ready to make an abatement of 1,500 gulden from the sum of 8,000 gulden, which was due as the half-year's contribution; the 6,500 gulden were to be paid on the festival of St. John.[1] As regards the salary of the Rabbi, which was the subject of the second petition, he made an abatement of 20 ducats. Thirdly, he allowed the same amount to be taken off the rent of the dye duty.

When I read this, I called together my partners in the lease, and I looked into their accounts and registers. After examining the money that was available in cash we saw that there was no possibility of getting even the amount which we had to pay after such a great deduction. I was very angry, seeing that nobody would assist me after my pleading had been successful in obtaining this large abatement. What (I wondered) should we say on St. John's day if the balance of the rent were not forthcoming for the

[1] 24th June 1767.

landlord? I and my partners were not sure of being able
to raise this sum on credit. I raised my eyes to the heights
and asked; "Whence will come my help? It will come
from God who created heaven and earth. God is almighty,
and He does not reject the seed of Israel, and He will
not fail to perform miracles and wondrous works to support them in time of trouble."[1]

The wealthy and powerful lease-holders of the salt-
springs at Bolechow, at Cissow[2] and at Lisowice, R. Isaac,
son-in-law of R. Moses, a member of our community, and
R. Mendel, son of R. Judah Loeb of Stryi, became very
jealous when they learned that we had received great
mercy on the part of the landlord. They both approached
me with the request that I should compose another petition to the landlord in their name. They sent R. Joseph,
son of R. Seinwel, who had mixed with the nobles and
knew the details of their request, to explain to me the
particulars, so that the petition should be written properly
and in a manner worthy of such a landlord. R. Joseph
said to me: "The leaseholders of the salt-springs are not
asking for an allowance from the landlord's treasury, and
are willing to pay the whole amount of the lease of the
salt-springs. In view, however, of the bad times and the
rise in prices, they find it impossible to get from the
peasants the money for the salt which has been sold to
them on credit. The peasants are unable to pay anything
on St. John's day, before the new crops are gathered. At
present they are still away, trying to sell the salt which
they took from the salt-springs. The lease-holders therefore ask the landlord to postpone payment from St. John's
day to that of St. Michael,[3] which is at the end of the
summer. That will be the right time to collect their debts
from the peasants, and the lease-holders will then be able

[1] Combination of various Biblical phrases.

[2] Village 7 km. south-east of Bolechow. Anciently there were salt-springs
at Cissow, but they have been neglected since 1791. See *Geographical Dictionary* (P.), vol. I.

[3] 29th September.

to pay the balance left over from St. John's day." I wrote
out all this properly and fittingly; and it occurred to me
that it might be useful for us to obtain help in the same
way. So I wrote a petition in the name of the Elders of the
whole population of our town, Gentile and Jewish alike, to
the effect that the Elders asked the landlord to be gracious
and to have compassion on the poor people of both the
Gentile and Jewish communities, who had been compelled
to take from the mills in that year at high prices much
corn and wheat, and other commodities necessary for the
maintenance of their hungry families. Owing to the bad
times these poor people could not repay their debts during
the summer, before the new crops were harvested. The
Elders of both communities, therefore, appealed to the
benevolence of the landlord to give an order that the
payment of the lease should be delayed until St. Michael's
day. The Judge of the town and the members of the
Municipal Council signed the petition with their names
and sealed it with the town's seal; the Elders of the
Jewish community and some of its members also signed
this petition.

. . . having heard how fluently and beautifully I spoke
Polish, he asked R. Isaac Zubri, his agent: "Why is it
that among you Jews living in such a large city as Lemberg no one speaks Polish so fluently as this young man,
who has as great a command of the language as any
of us?" The noble at once gave me five Dutch ducats for
ten pots of wine on condition that I should not sell from
this cask until he had taken the ten pots he bought, and,
that in addition he should be at liberty to require the
whole cask if he so wished. And it did indeed happen
so; this noble drank the whole cask and purchased some
other wines. Whenever he came to Lemberg after this,
he did not go to other merchants, but bought only from
us. Let us, however, return to our subject.

I brought the five ducats to my brother, and he was
very pleased, for six weeks had passed since he had come
to Lemberg, and none of his wines had been sold. He
therefore asked me to send the horse back to Bolechow,
and to remain with him at Lemberg to help him in the
sale of the wines. I accordingly remained at Lemberg,
and stood guard at the entrance to the building in which
the wines were stored. One day a gentleman came up
to me and asked: "Why do you stand here?" Whereupon
I replied: "I am looking for customers for good Hungarian
wines which we have in the cellars of this house." Then
he said: "I am also a good customer for good wines.
Show me the samples, that I may test their value, and I
will buy what I need." I brought the samples; we agreed
on a price, and he bought his wine from me so long as
he stayed at Lemberg. He was a Gentile, a German by
birth, employed by the firm of the wine trader Dietrich,
at Warsaw. He said to me: "If you wish it I could be
of great service to you, so that you would sell all your
wines in a week." Now he was book-keeper to the merchant Dietrich at Warsaw, where the nobles from all
the Polish provinces met during the Diet and on other
occasions. Most of the nobles had not sufficient money
to meet the expenses at Warsaw, and contracted debts,
which they promised to repay in Lemberg during the
time of the Fairs. So this book-keeper had come here to
Lemberg to collect those debts, as the nobles used to
bring to the Fairs all the money which they got from
their rents, and some of them would buy or sell properties, lend money and pay back debts contracted during
the past year. When some of these nobles saw this book-
keeper, they asked: "Herr Dietrich,[1] what are you doing
here at Lemberg?" The book-keeper replied: "I have
brought good Hungarian wines here to sell retail; they
are stored in the house of the Carmelite friars." He said
this because he did not like to put them to shame by

---

[1] They apparently called the book-keeper by the name of his principal.

saying that he had come to claim their debts. The nobles
on hearing this sent their servants with vessels and money
to obtain good wine for their masters, and the book-keeper
called out to me, (addressing me as his agent): "Give
wine to this and that gentleman from the cask you know
for cash, and enter the amount on the register in proper
order." In this way ten casks of wine were sold retail
in a week. The remainder of the goods were sold during
the same time by the whole cask.

As this Gentile had promised the nobles to furnish
them with wine, he did not want me to leave the house
and go about, because every moment servants were coming
from the nobles to buy wine. We had no separate room
in that house apart from the wine-cellars, so the book-
keeper obtained permission from a Frenchman, with whom
he shared a room, for me to stay with them all day in
their room. This Frenchman had arranged his wares there
in proper order, as is the way of such merchants. He was
a man of great means, a native of Paris, in France, and
named Fival, and he owned a shop full of various valuable
goods in the town of Lublin. This shop was under the
management of a clerk, whilst he himself, Fival, brought
many of his wares to Lemberg at the time of the Fairs,
accompanied by two junior clerks. One was twenty years
old, a native of Paris and named Carie; he did not understand any language but French. This Carie is still living
in Lemberg, is a member of the Municipal Council, and
owns a house built of bricks and a shop opposite the
Catholic Church. The other Clerk was a boy of seven-
teen, born at Leipzig and named Jacob John Labadie.
He knew three languages — French, German and Polish.
When he learned that I had some knowledge of Polish
and Latin, and that I was eager to learn to write and
speak German, this young man asked me: "Are you well
versed in Hebrew?" I replied: "Surely! I am a Hebrew
by birth, and learned our holy Hebrew language in
accordance with the Law, as is the custom of every
Jew." Whereupon Labadie said: "I will teach you our

German language on condition that you will teach me
to write and speak Hebrew." Immediately he wrote for
me the letters of the German alphabet; and I took the
pen from his hand and wrote a second alphabet beneath
after the pattern and the form of the first. Labadie was
very astonished, for when I wrote for him the Hebrew
alphabet he had to write it three times before he was
able to grasp the character of the Hebrew letters from
the examples I had set before him. He also saw that I
was versed in Polish. He was very pleased to teach me
the German letters and grammar, and wrote out for me
many proverbs in good German in a beautiful hand. I
on my side taught him the square Hebrew characters and
punctuation, and after he had learnt these from an alphabet printed at Zolkiew,[1] I had to buy him a prayer-book,
as I saw that he was very anxious to know Hebrew.
During a short time, that is in one week, I acquired a
good knowledge of the German tongue, and this Gentile
made a good start in the study of Hebrew. The merchant
Fival told us afterwards how a Jewish innkeeper, in whose
inn they stayed one night on their journey back from
Lemberg, presented them with a bill on which he had made
a note in Hebrew, for his own information, that a fowl
costs 15 *grosz*,[2] whereas he charged his guests one gulden,
and Labadie had noticed this. Fival was very surprised
that the young man had managed to learn such a difficult language in a short time, and that I had enabled
him to understand so much. Fival also told us that when
this youth returned to Leipzig to his father, a wealthy
man, he announced his disinclination to devote himself to
trade. His parents were willing to buy him a position in
the army, that is, to obtain for him a captaincy, but this
also he refused, as his sole aim was to give himself up
to the study of science and languages. Particularly he

---

[1] Town north of Lemberg. Since 1690 there had been a Hebrew printing
works there. See Barącz, *Reminiscences of the Town of Zolkiew* (P.), 1852.

[2] Half a gulden.

endeavoured to improve himself in Hebrew, until he had
fully mastered this language, and also the Arabian and
Babylonian tongues. After a few years he was appointed
to be Princidal, that is Professor, of Oriental languages
in the Academy of Leipzig.[1] At that time a book was
published in the German tongue at Leipzig, a translation
from the English. The author of it, a scholar named
Prideaux, lived in London.[2] In that work he described
and explained well the history of the nations which were
the neighbours of the Children of Israel, namely, those of
the Kingdoms of Assyria, Babylon, Persia, Media, Greece,
Macedonia and Antioch, also the Empire of Rome, which
arose after these nations, and how they fought against
Israel. Prideaux explained how the prophecies of the
Prophets were all fulfilled with regard to those peoples.
All that he wrote is true, as may be seen in the Holy
Books which we possess. The pastor Labadie sent me
this book, published in two volumes, and asked me (in
return) for some thoroughly tanned Transsylvanian lamb-
skins, which I forwarded to him through a German merchant, Schultz, a wealthy and well-known business man
then in Lemberg, who had brought me the book. This
Schultz, when he saw the book, paid me a *reichsthaler*
to let him read it, and also told some other merchants
the contents of the book, and they all paid a *reichsthaler*

---

[1] This statement is probably incorrect. According to G. Erler, *Jüngere
Matrikel der Universität Leipzig (1559—1809)*, vol. III, p. 225, Labadie
matriculated at the University of Leipzig in 1753. Ber made his acquaintance,
as we gather later from the narrative, before 1750. The matricula runs as
follows: "Labadie, Joh. Christ. Bendaw, Budissa P. i. 18. V. 1753." Budissa P.
means that he was a native of Bautzen (in Saxony, not of Leipzig, as Ber
asserts) and of Polish nationality. Ber mentions, it will be remarked, that
Labadie knew Polish. In response to my enquiry the Director of the
Leipzig University Library informs me that Labadie was neither Magister
nor Professor at that University. A few lines below Labadie is described
as "pastor."

[2] The first German translation of Prideaux' *Old and New Testament etc.*,
appeared as long ago as 1726. Ber must, therefore, have had in mind a
later edition.

each for permission to read it, viz., the merchants Blechner, Kutschera, Kreisel and Meissner, the last-named a book-keeper at the storehouse of the firm of Zinkiewicz. After they had all read the book it was returned to me, and I have it to this day. Now let us return to our subject.

We completed the sale of all the wines in a short time, and my brother, Aryeh Loeb, gave me a salary for my trouble and in addition the empty casks with the lees which were sold retail. I told my brother that all this would not satisfy me unless he would go with me once more to Hungary to buy wine, and give me a share in the business. He agreed to this proposal, when we re-turned home from Lemberg. We started immediately on our journey to Hungary, and reached Tokay in time for the Purim Festival in 510 (22d March, 1750). There we bought over 30 casks of old wine, which we decided at once to carry to Poland. Besides this my brother bought from the Greek trader, Lazar Janos,[1] a prosperous and well-known merchant, 60 casks of the vintage of 509 (1749), which were stored in the wine-cellars of Count Francis Dalay. Moreover, my brother left on the premises of the same Lazar Janos 12 casks of wine made from dry grapes, on which nothing had been paid, but for which my brother received a document saying that the wines were sold to him. I sealed all the casks with my brother's seal, and we returned home with the 30 casks, after the Passover, to Lemberg, where we stored them in the wine-cellars of the afore-mentioned monastery.

At that time there took place at Lemberg the last attack by the students. It has always been a plague in the community of Lemberg that in the course of dissensions and quarrels, which usually arose between a Jew and a student of the College on some small matter the other

---

[1] In Hungarian the surname usually precedes the personal name. This John Lazar was one of the prominent wine-merchants of Tokay, as we learn from another contemporary source. See A. Fournier, *Handel und Verkehr in Ungarn und Polen um die Mitte des XVIII. Jahrhunderts*, in *Archiv für Österreichische Geschichtsforschung*, vol. 69, p. 370.

students, of noble parentage, would rush into the Jewish quarter, beat and kill the Jews and plunder their goods. The Jews had to flee in order to save their lives, and the students looted and carried away all possible belongings of the Jews. But let us return to our subject.

The wines we had then brought to Lemberg were sold at a good price by the 17th of the month of *Tammuz* in 510 (21st July 1750), on which date no cask was left with us. On that day we departed from Lemberg for home, via the township of Strzeliska,[1] where my brother's wife Rachel when she was with us at Lemberg had expressed a wish to stop in order to pay a visit to her family, namely, to her brother R. Joshua, a distinguished and renowned merchant, connected with Danzig, his sons and the other members of the family. On the night of the 19th *Tammuz* (23rd July) we reached the village of Bortniki, near the banks of the river Dniester, where we stopped to pass the night. On that night a respected member of our community, R. Raphael, was murdered in the village of Brzozowa, in the vicinity of Bolechow.[2] He had built a house in the main street of our town in the very year of his death, but he was not spared to consecrate it, as the murderers fell upon him by night and killed him. R. Raphael left no children, and the house was inherited by his wife, who later married R. Itamar, a scholar and capable *mohel*,[3] skilled in his profession. After his death the house was inherited by R. Michel, son of R. Seinwel, the brother-in-law of the widow of the martyr R. Raphael. Now it belongs to R. Seinwel, R. Michel's son.

But we must return to our subject, and tell how we made our preparations for travelling to Hungary for the purpose of carrying away the wine which we had already bought. We hired waggons drawn by oxen in the villages

---

[1] Township in the district of Bobrka, in Eastern Galicia.
[2] Situated in the mountains at a distance of 19 km. from Bolechow.
[3] See footnote 4 on p. 71.

in the vicinity of Munkacs, and arrived with them at Tokay,
where the 72 casks of choice wine had been stored. Further
we purchased other 40 casks of good wine. The waggons
arrived, and the casks were loaded on them. They came
to the ford of the Theiss on the side of Tokay, where
there is now a large bridge, built at great expense by
the Emperor. At that time, however, the river had to be
forded or crossed in boats. It happened that our waggoners
when staying on the bank of the Theiss near Tokay became
very drunk from indulging in much wine. I went to urge
them to hurry and cross the river before the day ended,
as there was no pasture for their cattle near the town,
and night was coming on. One of the waggoners approached me to embrace me, as is the manner of drunken
people. He said: "If you knew the taste of the wine we
have drunk to-day you would not move us from here."
The smell of the wine which came from his mouth made
me aware that it must have been old. The carter further
said that this wine was sold at 7 *kreuzer* the quarter. I
immediately went to speak to the Jewish shop-keeper who
had sold that wine, R. Joseph by name, who had his business at Tokay in the house of the noble Patay. R. Joseph
told me that that wine had been preserved in barrels,
100 of which remained after the death of the noble, but
the wine had fermented, and Patay's widow therefore had
to sell it at a low price to R. Elieser the Great of the
town of Karoly — so called because there lived at the
same place a certain R. Elieser Ashkenasi, surnamed the
Little. This R. Elieser the Great received the 100 barrels
for 100 ducats on a year's credit, and gave them for retail
sale to the shopkeepers throughout the villages, as he
held the leases of many inns belonging to the noble lady
Patay. I learned from R. Joseph that 8 barrels of that
wine had been brought to him; so I immediately went
to his house, entered the cellar, and tasted the wine. I
found six barrels full and of a very good quality, and
these barrels I corked up, as is the custom, in order
to avoid a second visit to the cellar. I then informed my

brother, who negotiated with R. Joseph, and agreed to take the six barrels for 14 ducats. The waggoners came, took the barrels on their shoulders, and loaded them on to their waggons.

We arrived safely in Lemberg with about 120 casks of wine of a very choice quality, and sold them all at a good profit. During the Fairs most of the wines in the casks were sold, but the six barrels remained until the clergy of the episcopate and the nobles, who were accustomed to old wines, learned of the existence of those barrels, and then the contents of four barrels were sold to them retail at a ducat per bottle. Subsequently the four empty barrels were filled with good wines, and we sold them to Jewish traders, who carried them to Danzig and Leipzig. The remaining two barrels were stored until after the Passover, when Count Potocki, the *voyevoda* of Kiev,[1] took up his residence with the Carmelite friars. The Gentiles were then celebrating the Year of Jubilee,[2] in which year, in their opinion, all sins were to be forgiven, and Count Potocki had come to Lemberg to pray God to forgive his sins. He was bound to visit daily various churches, where he offered prayers, and as the house of the Carmelites was in a central position, it was chosen for his residence, and everything that he needed was brought there, including a barrel of old wine purchased from the Jesuits for the sum of 136 ducats. The Count's servant, who supervised the wine-cellar, asked me for a funnel with which to fill the decanters, which were served at the table, and told me how valuable was that barrel of wine obtained from the monks of the Jesuit monastery. I gave him the funnel, and went with him down to the cellar, where he let me taste the wine, which, he said, was grown in 1700. I tasted the wine, and remarked that we had two barrels of wine that were also very fine. The

---

[1] Count Stanislaus Potocki was *voyevoda* of Kiev in 1748—1754.

[2] The Catholic Church has ordained every 25th year to be observed as a Jubilee Year, which lasts from Christmas to Christmas.

servant asked for samples, which were tried by the Count
and pleased him. Then my brother, R. Aryeh Loeb, was
called to the Count in order to settle the price. He said:
"As it is well-known to all that you, My Lord, be your
Lordship exalted, grant favours to our brethren of Israel,
who are spread in great numbers over your estates, and
as God has decided that I should serve your Highness,
I will sell the two barrels of wine without any profit.
I am prepared to make an abatement of 200 ducats,
taking as a basis the price of 136 ducats per barrel,
which the friars received, although the wine in my barrels
is a little better in colour and in taste. I therefore offer
them to your Highness for 72 ducats." The Count was
pleased with these words, and expressed his gratitude
for the reduction of the price. He ordered 72 ducats
to be paid immediately to my brother, who received
this amount in coins of the right weight. The barrels
were sealed with the Count's seal.

In the month of *Ab*, in 511 (23rd July — 22nd August
1751), we proceeded again to Tokay and Tarczal, and
made a purchase of more than 100 casks of wine, all of
good taste and at reasonable prices. We sold this quantity
at a considerable profit during the Fairs, in 512 (1752).
There had remained with us from the three seasons, that
is three years, 30 barrels or 5 casks of wine made of
dry grapes, called *Ausbruch*, very sweet, and therefore unfit
for the nobility to drink and impossible to sell. These
barrels were left for storage in the farm of the noble
Bielski, the Master of the Hunts of the Crown, which
was named *"Dworek Metropolitanski"* and was held on
lease by R. Moses Shnapik, a respectable and honest
person. We handed to him the key of the cellar, that he
might look after our goods from time to time and pre-
serve them from damage. The other wines which we
had bought were afterwards stored in the cellars of the
aforesaid brick house of the Carmelite friars, opposite the
gate of Halicz, where it was proposed that they should
be brought for sale as in previous years. The friars let

us also have an apartment for ourselves, so that we could live in the same building, at the second entrance to the right of the general entrance. Now-a-days there is in this room, where I spent the nights during 25 years, the Imperial Post Office, and through the windows of that room all the people of the country have for years received their letters from the Lemberg post.

One day there came to stay in R. Moses Shnapik's house a Commissioner who had been sent from St. Petersburg, from the Muscovite country, to Hungary for the purchase of Tokay wine. R. Moses, on learning his business, said to this Commissioner: "Sir, there are in my house many good wines for sale, and they are of Tokay." Whereupon the Commissioner replied: "Well, I will buy them if they are choice and fit to be put on the table of kings." R. Moses then came at three o'clock in the morning and awakened me and forced me to rise, and I went with him to talk to the Commissioner, who, as I saw, was really a Russian official, being accompanied by ten soldiers of the army of the Russian Emperor. The Commissioner went with me to the cellar, tasted the wine and found it suitable. There were in the cellar altogether 15 casks and some barrels of such a size that two of them equalled one cask. In the cellar the Commissioner immediately agreed to pay 11 ducats per barrel, but I asked 20, or in any case not less than 18 ducats.

When the day dawned we went to say our morning prayers. In the meantime a Greek wine-trader, named Ignatius, called on the Commissioner, who knew him fairly well. The Commissioner told him that he had tasted our wines, and was prepared to pay 11 ducats for them, but that the Jew was not willing to sell them under a very high price. The Greek then remarked: "Sir, you must know that there are here at Lemberg other Jews who bring wines to sell. Many of our traders have purchased very choice wines at 8 ducats the barrel only. In the large courtyard of Prince Czartoryski, the *voyevoda* of the province of Red Ruthenia, are many cellars full of

Hungarian wines brought here by Jewish traders from
Skole, which are being sold cheaper than the other." The
Commissioner listened to the Greek, and got ready to go
and see these wines of the traders of Skole, and turning
to me said: "Come with me also. I will buy from them
and also from you all your wines after we have agreed
as to the price." I followed the Commissioner, and just
as we arrived at the cellar, we met R. Judah Loeb of
Skole, who then had in stock a considerable quantity of
wine. R. Judah said to the Commissioner: "If this Jewish
trader follows you to my cellar I shall not open it, neither
shall I show you my wines." When I heard this I said
to the Muscovite official: "I wish you all luck," and I
returned home, accompanied by R. Jacob Klimtser of
Skole. Before I reached my place the Commissioner ran
in haste from there by another street, and immediately
sent for me in order to continue negotiations. I then
observed that he was willing to buy my wines, but that
the Greek Ignatius had misled him, telling him that Hungarian wines were being sold at Lemberg very cheaply,
namely, at 8 ducats per barrel, and had thus made him
reluctant to pay for my wines in accordance with their
value: the more so as I was then only 23 years old.[1]
My elder brother was then at home at Bolechow, having
left me alone to look after the wines at Lemberg, which
were stored in the two cellars of the brick house of the
monks and were ready to be sold retail in quarters. We
had also 30 barrels of good wine in a third cellar in the
court-yard of the noble Bielski. All these wines were
under my charge, the keys of the cellars were in my
hands, and I had the full right to sell, as I knew by the
ledgers which were in my possession the purchase price
and the cost of transport, and therefore knew what to
demand for them. I decided in my mind not to sell any

---

[1] This is a slip of the pen. Below Ber speaks of his elder son Joshua,
a boy of 9 years, as having been with him in Lemberg, and Ber's second
marriage took place in 1742, when he was 19 years old.

cask under 30 ducats and any *antal* (or barrel) under 15.
But the Commissioner wanted to buy such wines cheap,
relying on the Greek merchant Ignatius, and stayed a
whole day in order to deceive me; but I was firm in my
demand for 18 ducats per barrel. So he started to take
his departure with his retinue, and when they had actually
left the inn in their carriage, they asked me to tell them
my lowest price; but I replied that I still stood by my
words and demanded 18 ducats per barrel. Finally the
Commissioner, who was sitting in his carriage, called me
to him and agreed to give me 36 ducats per cask. I gave
him my hand, and the price was fixed; he returned to his
inn, and remained there over night, giving me 50 ducats
as a deposit. The contract was written, and he ordered
new hoops to be put on the barrels after he had sealed
them with his seal. The rest of the money he undertook
to pay, according to the contract, in ducats of full weight
when the waggons should be sent to take the wine.

The Commissioner told me that he was going from
here to Tokay to purchase more wine there. I then
said to him: "Sir, when you arrive at Tokay would you
have the goodness to pay to the Greek merchant, Lazar
Janos, 160 ducats in accordance with a promissory note
which he holds with the signature of my brother, R. Aryeh
Loeb." The Commissioner was good enough to promise
to carry out my request, and duly paid the money; and
the merchant Lazar Janos wrote and signed on the torn
promissory note that he had received the whole sum due,
that is, 160 ducats. The Commissioner sent me 240 ducats
besides the deposit, which together with the sum paid to
the Greek amounted to 450 ducats, so that he paid for
30 barrels at 15 ducats each.[1] The profit on this transaction was half the sum for which we sold the wine, that
is to say 225 ducats: in other words, I gained a ducat for a
ducat. This sale I managed to effect myself, as my brother

---

[1] But we have just been told that the Muscovite commissioner agreed
to pay 18 ducats per barrel.

had remained at Bolechow and left me at Lemberg with
the wines stored in the cellars. I had no servant; only
my elder son, Joshua, then a boy of nine years, was with
me. We had brought him to Lemberg to seek a cure for
the disease he had in his leg. Although he was unable
to move about, he understood everything about my household affairs, and was intelligent enough to look after what
was going on indoors and in the cellar. I had to take care
of him and to provide the necessary things for the cure
of his disease. Also I had to manage alone the whole retail
business on the premises of the friars, and besides this I
carried through the transaction with the Muscovite officer.

At that time a wine-trader of Skole, R. Jacob Klimtser,
went to stay with R. Moses Shnapik. R. Jacob was related to me, having been a grandson of my aunt, and
therefore my first cousin once removed. He observed all
my negotiations with the Muscovite, and asked me: "How
do you share with your brother?" I replied: "I take a
third of the profit." In fact my brother had promised that
I should have the fourth part. I gathered from R. Jacob's
question that he was eager to form a partnership with
me in the wine-business.

But I must say that even this fourth part was not given
to me, for my brother and his wife, Rachel, altered the
commission. Rachel was envious of my fortune, and afraid
lest my brother should enter into more intimate connections
with me. She was hoping for his death, and though she
was liberally provided for in accordance with her marriage-
contract, she was afraid of my knowing anything about
her husband's estate. She was jealous of my wife, Leah,
who was well-known to everybody, both Jews and Gentiles,
as an exemplary woman. Seeing her becoming obsessed
by jealousy and hatred, I decided to dissolve partnership
with my brother, with whom I had carried on business
for two and half years. We had been three times to Tokay
to buy large quantities of wine. From the account books
which I had kept since I commenced business with my
brother, I made out the expenses of our journeys to Hun-

gary and those connected with the sale of our stocks at
Lemberg. Further, I added the expenses incurred by my
brother on his journey to Brody, after the sale of the wines
was completed. He had spent there a considerable amount
of money, more than 2,000 gulden, in buying dresses and
jewels for his wife. Amongst other things he bought a
set of robes of the Queen of Prussia for 80 ducats; they
were made of beautiful silk — fine brocade — and embroidered with real gold, and their like had never been
seen before in our country. My brother promised to give
my wife a portion of the silk for a skirt or for a cloak.
but when he came home, his wife took it all and did not
give us "from a tread to a sandal-thong".[1] In spite of
this, I allowed all these expenses of my brother. After
deducting the initial capital brought into the business
there remained a clear profit of 14,000 gulden, and out
of it all I received 80 ducats as my share.

I then learned that traders of Skole had brought wines
from Hungary, and I thought it would be good if I purchased some casks of them and carried them to Lemberg
to sell them to our customers of the nobility, before my
brother arrived with his wines. Accordingly I went to Skole
and stayed there with R. Jacob Klimtser. I tasted the wines
of many traders, but could not come to any agreement
as to the price. I stayed the night, and in the morning
saddled my horse and went to take leave of the host of
the inn, Jacob Klimtser. He was in bed enjoying a morning sleep, but when he was awakened he rose at once
and took hold of the bridle of the horse, asking me not
to go until after the morning prayer in the synagogue.
He went immediately to speak with the wine traders.
One of them, R. Manes, had 11 casks of good wine; we
agreed as to the price and I paid him from my pocket.
Then R. Jacob unbosomed himself and said to me: "My
friend, R. Ber, let us be partners. You will share the wines
which you have bought from R. Manes, and I for my

---

[1] Gen. 14[23].

part will share 13 casks of my own wines, which are a little better, as you must know since you have tasted them. Then we will go to Lemberg, and perhaps the Almighty will help us to sell our goods before the other traders arrive there." I consented to his suggestion, and a contract of partnership was drawn up between us. We brought our stocks to Lemberg in the month of *Elul* 512, (1752) and stored them in the brick house of the Carmelite friars, at the same place where I had sold those wines which I held with my brother.

There, at Lemberg, I purchased from R. Judah Loeb Lischwitser, who had just come to sell wines of his brother-in-law, R. Naḥman, 18 casks of excellent wine. This R. Judah Loeb was not accustomed to speak to the nobles, and was therefore not in a position to sell them wine; in consequence of this he had to let us have the wine at cost-price. From this purchase we sold several casks, and we left the remainder at Lemberg, under the control of my learned brother, R. Axelrod Bendet. My partner, R. Jacob, left his wines with his brother, R. Isaac. We — my partner and myself — collected the takings from the sales and made preparations for our departure to Hungary. We reached Miskolcz early in the month of *Marḥeshvan*, in 512,[1] (9th October — 8th November 1752) where we purchased a large quantity of mediocre wine, the old sorts of *máslás* not being available. The Greek merchant Sambek had some of those old wines, but he was not willing to sell even one cask . . . .

[1] Should be 513 (1753).

APPENDIX [1]

. . . He (Prideaux) interpreted this prophecy as referring to their false Redeemer, for (he argued) since the coming of Jesus rulership has departed from Judah. Some Jews have tried to refute this interpretation by a number of arguments, proving it impossible that our forefather Jacob's prophecy expressed in that phrase could allude to Jesus the Nazarene. The priest, Jacob Radlinski, canon of Lublin, wrote much on this matter in a book, full of lies, entitled "Rab Shemuel", in Polish "Samuel Rabin".[2] This book abounds in mistakes and shameful falsehoods, which are not worth writing down or quoting to reasonable people. The third edition of it appeared at Lublin in 1753 of the Christian Era. In the same year it came into my hands, and I read it. Besides this book, "Samuel Rabin", I read also some more of their theological writings dealing with the Jews, in which they malign and slander the Jewish people and our holy Oral Law, which we have by tradition. All these books I read with grief in my heart, but I acquired much knowledge of their doctrines. I discerned in their arguments great errors and obduracy. Moreover, I became acquainted with all the fables and miracles in which they believed, things which never really existed.

---

[1] On the first 42 pages of the manuscript we find some paragraphs dealing with the author's time. In his translation of Humphrey Prideaux' *Old and New Testament, etc.*, Ber came upon a statement of that author that the prophecy in Gen. Chap. 49, V. 10: "The sceptre shall not depart from Judah etc." had been realized with the coming of Jesus.

[2] Jacob Paul Radliński, priest, theological writer, poet and historian, d. 1762. The full title of his book, to which Ber alludes, is: *Prawda chrześcijanska, to jest list Rabina Samuela do Rabina Izaka przekład z łacińskiego z dodatkami tłumacza* (Lublin 1732, 2 d. ed. 1733, 3 d. ed. 1753). See R. Estreicher, *Polish Bibliography* (P.). This book was one of the sources of the anti-Semitic pamphleteers in Poland.

The reward of my labour in that distasteful study was given to me and to the whole of Israel on the occasion of the great and famous dispute which took place at Lemberg between all Israel, on the one side, and the evil sect of the believers in Shabbetai Zebi, be his name extinguished, on the other side. I acted as the interpreter from Polish into our holy tongue and from Hebrew into Polish. I reported and wrote the questions as well as the replies, which were made by the learned and venerable Rabbi Ḥayyim Ha-Cohen Rappaport, in 1759, in the Great Church at Lemberg. I will, God willing, deal in detail with this subject, in its place.[1]

In all this affair I served the truth and behaved with self-confidence, as I explained in the beginning of my introduction;[2] and all the Gentiles, the nobles and the other people saw that I was accustomed to read their books and to understand the contents of them, and was acquainted with most of their doctrines and the history of the world. One of the nobles presented me with a book of an Italian author, Giovanni Botero Benesius, which was a translation from Italian into Polish made by Lencicius, a priest. This work was entitled "Teatrum Świata" and its second edition was published at Cracow, in 1659.[3] The noble said that this author (Botero) wrote much about . . . . . and that I should read it to know more of what had happened to our people of Israel.[4] . . .

---

[1] This interesting episode is related by Ber in his *Dibré Binah*. See Introduction, p. 42.

[2] The meaning is obscure. Possibly Ber alludes to his opening speech at the Dispute.

[3] Giovanni Benesius Botero — historian and geographer (1540—1617). His famous book *Relazioni universali* (Rome, 1592—1595) was published many times and in various languages. There were three Polish editions, the first in 1609 under the title *Relatiae powszechne abo Nowiny pospolite, etc.*, the second in 1613 under a new title: *Teatrum Świata wszystkiego etc.*, and the third in 1659 under the same title, which means *Theatre of the World*.

[4] This page of the manuscript is defective. We abstain from further translation of unconnected words. What follows is a short description of the book and several extracts from it in Hebrew.

INDEX.

THE JEWISH PEOPLE

HISTORY • RELIGION • LITERATURE

AN ARNO PRESS COLLECTION

Agus, Jacob B. **The Evolution of Jewish Thought:** From
Biblical Times to the Opening of the Modern Era. 1959

Ber of Bolechow. **The Memoirs of Ber of Bolechow**
(1723-1805). Translated from the Original Hebrew MS. with an
Introduction, Notes and a Map by M[ark] Vishnitzer. 1922

Berachya. **The Ethical Treatises of Berachya, Son of Rabbi**
Natronai Ha-Nakdan: Being the Compendium and the Masref.
Now edited for the First Time from MSS. at Parma and Munich
with an English Translation, Introduction, Notes, etc. by
Hermann Gollancz. 1902

Bloch, Joseph S. **My Reminiscences.** 1923

Bokser, Ben Zion, **Pharisaic Judaism in Transition:** R. Eliezer
the Great and Jewish Reconstruction After the War with Rome.
1935

Dalman, Gustaf. **Jesus Christ in the Talmud, Midrash, Zohar,**
and the Liturgy of the Synagogue. Together with an
Introductory Essay by Heinrich Laible. Translated and Edited
by A. W. Streane. 1893

Daube, David. **The New Testament and Rabbinic Judaism.** 1956

Davies, W. D. **Christian Origins and Judaism.** 1962

Engelman, Uriah Zevi. **The Rise of the Jew in the Western**
World: A Social and Economic History of the Jewish People
of Europe. Foreword by Niles Carpenter. 1944

Epstein, Louis M. **The Jewish Marriage Contract:** A Study
in the Status of the Woman in Jewish Law. 1927

Facets of Medieval Judaism. 1973. New Introduction by
Seymour Siegel

The Foundations of Jewish Life: Three Studies. 1973

Franck, Adolph. **The Kabbalah, or, The Religious Philosophy**
of the Hebrews. Revised and Enlarged Translation [from the
French] by Dr. I. Sossnitz. 1926

Goldman, Solomon. **The Jew and The Universe.** 1936

Gordon, A. D. **Selected Essays.** Translated by Frances Burnce
from the Hebrew Edition by N. Teradyon and A. Shohat,
with a Biographical Sketch by E. Silberschlag. 1938

Ha-Am, Achad (Asher Ginzberg). **Ten Essays on Zionism and**
Judaism. Translated from the Hebrew by Leon Simon. 1922.
New Introduction by Louis Jacobs

Halevi, Jehudah. **Selected Poems of Jehudah Halevi.**
Translated into English by Nina Salaman, Chiefly from the
Critical Text Edited by Heinrich Brody. 1924

Heine, Heinrich. **Heinrich Heine's Memoir:** From His Works,
Letters, and Conversations. Edited by Gustav Karpeles;
English Translation by Gilbert Cannan. 1910. Two volumes in one

Heine, Heinrich. **The Prose Writings of Heinrich Heine.**
Edited, with an Introduction, by Havelock Ellis. 1887

Hirsch, Emil G[ustav]. **My Religion.** Compilation and
Biographical Introduction by Gerson B. Levi. **Including
The Crucifixion Viewed from a Jewish Standpoint:** A Lecture
Delivered by Invitation Before the "Chicago Institute for
Morals, Religion and Letters." 1925/1908

Hirsch, W. **Rabbinic Psychology:** Beliefs about the Soul
in Rabbinic Literature of the Talmudic Period. 1947

Historical Views of Judaism: Four Selections. 1973

Ibn Gabirol, Solomon. **Selected Religious Poems of Solomon Ibn
Gabirol.** Translated into English Verse by Israel Zangwill
from a Critical Text Edited by Israel Davidson. 1923

Jacobs, Joseph. **Jesus as Others Saw Him:** A Retrospect
A. D. 54. Preface by Israel Abrahams; Introductory Essay by
Harry A. Wolfson. 1925

Judaism and Christianity: Selected Accounts, 1892-1962.
1973. New Preface and Introduction by Jacob B. Agus

Kohler, Kaufmann. **The Origins of the Synagogue and
The Church.** Edited, with a Biographical Essay by H. G. Enelow.
1929

Maimonides Octocentennial Series, Numbers I-IV. 1935

Mann, Jacob. **The Responsa of the Babylonian Geonim as a
Source of Jewish History.** 1917-1921

Maritain, Jacques. **A Christian Looks at the Jewish Question.** 1939

Marx, Alexander. **Essays in Jewish Biography.** 1947

Mendelssohn, Moses. **Phaedon; or, The Death of Socrates.**
Translated from the German [by Charles Cullen]. 1789

Modern Jewish Thought: Selected Issues, 1889-1966. 1973.
New Introduction by Louis Jacobs

Montefiore, C[laude] G. **Judaism and St. Paul:** Two Essays. 1914

Montefiore, C[laude] G. **Some Elements of the Religious
Teaching of Jesus According to the Synoptic Gospels.** Being
the Jowett Lectures for 1910. 1910

Radin, Max. **The Jews Amongs the Greeks and Romans.** 1915

Ruppin, Arthur. **The Jews in the Modern World.** With an
Introduction by L. B. Namier. 1934

Smith, Henry Preserved. **The Bible and Islam;** or, The Influence
of the Old and New Testaments on the Religion of Mohammed.
Being the Ely Lectures for 1897. 1897

Stern, Nathan. **The Jewish Historico-Critical School of the
Nineteenth Century.** 1901

Walker, Thomas [T.] **Jewish Views of Jesus:** An Introduction
and an Appreciation. 1931. New Introduction by Seymour Siegel

Walter, H. **Moses Mendelssohn:** Critic and Philosopher. 1930

Wiener, Leo. **The History of Yiddish Literature in the
Nineteenth Century.** 1899

Wise, Isaac M. **Reminiscences.** Translated from the German and
Edited, with an Introduction by David Philipson. 1901